Learning Hiragana (Japanese Made Simple)

Learn how to read, write and speak Japanese, with Hiragana

A Beginner's Guide and Integrated Workbook

Dan Akiyama

JAPANESE FOR BEGINNERS | SYSTEMATIC LEARNING APPROACH

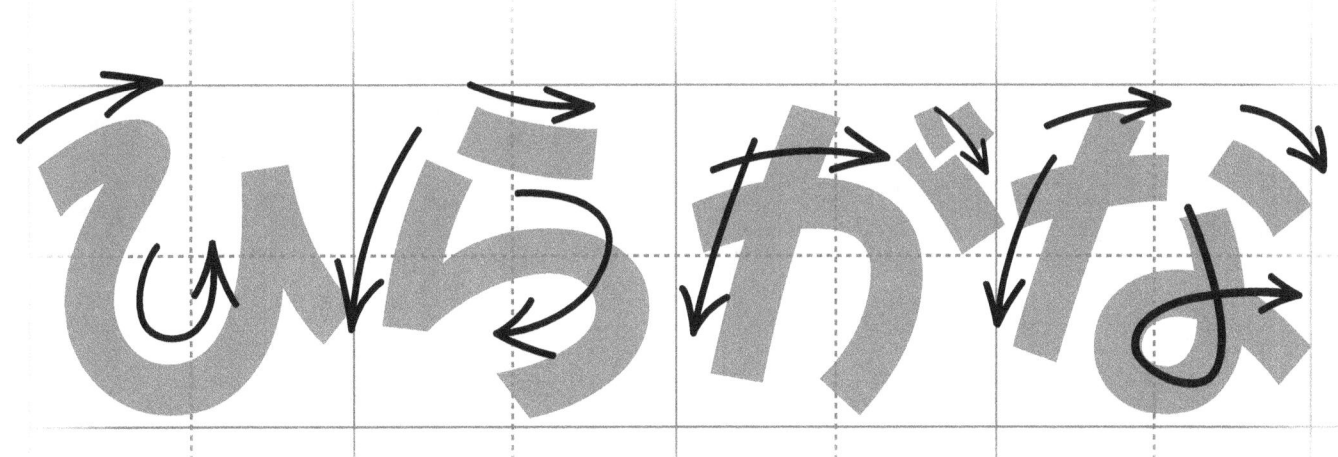

HIRAGANA
MADE SIMPLE®
READ, WRITE AND SPEAK JAPANESE

日本語

- Memorize the Hiragana *alphabet*
- Pronounce all the sounds in Japanese
- Develop powerful mnemonics
- Practice reading and writing
+ Extra study tools and templates

BEGINNER'S GUIDE + INTEGRATED WORKBOOK

DAN AKIYAMA

Learning Hiragana
Japanese Made Simple

Beginner's Guide and Integrated Workbook

by Dan Akiyama

ISBN: Print 978-1-7392387-2-8 (Paperback)
First Edition

**Copyright © 2022 by Dan Akiyama.
All Rights Reserved.**

No part of the content within this publication may be reproduced, duplicated, stored in a retrieval system, or transmitted in any form or by any means, electronic, mechanical, photocopying, recording, scanning, or otherwise, except as provided by United States of America copyright law and fair use, without the prior written permission of the Publisher and author. You are not permitted to amend, distribute, sell, use, paraphrase, or quote any part of this publication without the author and Publisher's consent.

Limit of Liability/Disclaimer of Warranty:
The author and Publisher make no representations or warranties with respect to the accuracy or completeness of the contents of this work and expressly disclaim all warranties, including, without limitation, warranties of fitness for a particular purpose. No warranty may be created or extended by sales or promotional materials.

The advice and strategies contained herein may not be suitable for every situation. This work is published and sold with the understanding that the Publisher is not engaged in rendering medical, legal, or other professional advice or services. If professional assistance is required, the services of a competent professional should be sought. Neither the Publisher nor the author shall be liable for any damages arising from the information contained within this publication.

The fact that an individual, organization, or website is referred to in this work as either a citation and/or potential source of further information does not mean that the author or Publisher endorses the information from the individual, organization, or website that may provide, or recommendations that they/it may make.

Furthermore, readers should be aware that any websites listed in this work may have changed or disappeared between when this publication was written and when it is read.

Contents

1 Introduction — 007
- Learning Japanese — 009
- Japanese 'Alphabets' — 011
- Writing Japanese — 013
- About Mnemonics — 016
- Syllables & 'Mora' — 017

2 Hiragana — 019
- Hiragana Chart — 021
- Learning Hiragana — 022

3 Additional Sounds — 095
- Voiced Consonants — 097
- Combination Kana — 098
- Double Letters — 100

4 Study Tools — 103
- Writing Templates — 104
- About the JLPT — 144
- Mini Flashcard Deck — 147
- Answer Key — 155

Note of Thanks — 157

/////////////////////////////// **PART 1**

Introduction

Welcome to the first workbook in the *Japanese Made Simple* series, *Learning Hiragana*. This set of books is designed to help you learn how to read, write, and pronounce Japanese, by simplifying the process and presenting information in a logical way. It's popularity as a new foreign language to learn is constantly growing, despite the challenges that surround the use of totally different characters to European languages.

The guided self-study materials in this workbook aim to help you reach your goals quickly, whatever your reason for studying Japanese. By the end of this workbook, you will have learned about the role that hiragana plays amongst Japanese, memorized how the different characters sound, and how to write each of them in the correct way.

About this Book

This book places emphasis on writing practice as a means to learn and remember these elementary characters. Most would probably concede that manual handwriting tends not to be required much in any language, since most of our communication and even work takes place online. Therefore, writing skills tend not to be a high priority when learning other foreign languages, such as French or Spanish. However, it plays a different role when you begin studying a foreign language with an entirely new set of characters or letters.

The activities in this workbook will develop your ability to write Japanese hiragana neatly, but their primary function is as a tool for learning and memorization. Writing and spaced repetition are simply some of the most effective tools for making information stick. They build muscle memory that will help you recognize and recall the sound or meaning of a character from shapes. Neat and tidy penmanship is an essential skill in Japanese anyway, and you will achieve this naturally as a bonus!

When learning how to write each new character and follow the correct stroke order, you should practice pronouncing the sounds that each symbol represents. The process of repeatedly writing characters and saying them out loud will help to attach sounds to the shapes you see. Space is also provided for the creation and recording of mnemonics - powerful tools for memorization - with examples and hints to help you each step of the way. Before long, you will be able to read and write Japanese using the hiragana script.

It is always good to begin immersing yourself in the language as soon as possible. Find ways to read, watch, or listen to Japanese language materials, even though you may not understand them. Hearing the sounds will make saying things aloud in Japanese feel less awkward and make pronunciations more natural-sounding.

How hard is it?

When you learn the right way, *Japanese is not that difficult*. The problems and frustrations that learners face are often caused by simply starting with the wrong strategy. It is easy to choose a difficult study route without knowing that there are other, better ways.

Without understanding how all the pieces go together, those who begin by learning only how to *say* a few random words or phrases will soon find confusion. This route is likely to waste a lot of time or discourage even the most eager learner, especially when the difficulty starts to ramp upwards.

Each aspect of Japanese works relatively logically, so it makes sense to take a systematic approach to your studies. If you want to learn Japanese efficiently, you must start with the basics.

Learning Japanese

With no, or very little knowledge, Japanese can seem difficult to learn. After all, it consists of many thousands of totally new and unique letters! That's why this workbook will start with only the essentials, and introduce extra information only when it will be helpful and useful. This chapter will begin with a quick assessment of what lies ahead.

At a really basic level, there are just three stages in the process and each subsequent level builds on the understanding and knowledge that you develop. Later stages are made easier with the information from previous ones and it must all be learned, so there is no practical way to skip ahead without adding difficulty or, eventually, coming back to the beginning:

1. Learning Kana

What: The kana *'alphabets'* represent sounds and enable you to read and pronounce all Japanese. Effectively, they allow everything else to be spelled out in a simplified way - but have lots of other uses.

How: Memorizing the shapes and pronunciations through repetition. There are two sets basic symbols and could take just a day or two. It is best not to rush here, as they are the foundation on which you will build everything else.

2. Acquiring Kanji Knowledge

What: Kanji are symbols that represent whole words, instead of sounds, so make up the largest part of Japanese. Some are simple, but lots are complex - and most have multiple meanings with alternate pronunciations. *A command of the kana scripts is a pre-requisite for kanji study.*

How: Due to the sheer volume, they inevitably take longer than learning kana. There are a variety of routes and methods, but do not have to be as tricky.

3. Adding Grammar

What: Equipped with kanji knowledge *(or a dictionary)*, you can understand lots of Japanese when you learn about sentence structure, how to make other word-forms, can recognize particles, and appreciate respectful speech.

How: Largely, memorizing and applying rules to your kanji knowledge; learn about verb conjugations and explore useful grammatical patterns found in everyday Japanese language. Reading practice is really helpful at this stage.

All of my workbooks are divided into sections to help structure your learning in the most effective way. This *Learning Hiragana* workbook consists of four parts, and should be approached in chronological order:

Section 1

An overview of the Japanese writing systems that will begin by explaining what each of the different *'alphabets'* or scripts are, and how they come together to form the language. You will also learn about the way that we read, write, and pronounce individual characters and fuller texts.

Section 2

The second chapter will teach you all about the **Hiragana,** the first of Japan's two phonetic *'alphabets,'* or syllabaries. The 46 basic characters are divided into groups of 'letters' with similar sounds, to make everything a little quicker. Here, you will learn how to write each symbol with the correct stroke order, and how they should sound when spoken. Each group ends with exercises that will help you to memorize the shapes and pronunciations you will have learned.

Section 3

Once you have mastered the basic characters, you will learn about the way that additional sounds are shown with extra written markings. The shapes you will have learned about up to this point will be re-used to write some extra, but fairly similar, pronunciation sounds. On completion of this section, there are no more Hiragana characters to learn.

Section 4

This section of the book consists of some useful study tools, including extra, blank grids for further writing practice. Generally, I would reccomend purchasing a separate notepad for practicing your Japanese, but these sheets may be handy for repetition of characters that you might have found particularly tricky.

Towards the rear of this chapter, and the book overall, I have included some double-sided pages of cut-out study tiles or *'flashcards'* which you can use to create a deck of helpful prompts for testing your memory. *Feel free to make copies if you prefer not to remove pages.* They might not be as large or durable as real 'cards', but they are nice to have without an extra cost, and work well as part of writing exercises. You could use them to check whether you remember the stroke order for hiragana in a randomized sequence.

The 'Alphabets'

You will encounter and use **four different types of characters** while learning the language, although *one is not strictly Japanese*. We will refer to each set as an *'alphabet'*, for ease, since that is a familiar concept that will simplify initial studies for an English-speaker. The *main* alphabets are **Hiragana, Katakana, and Kanji,** and they are frequently used together:

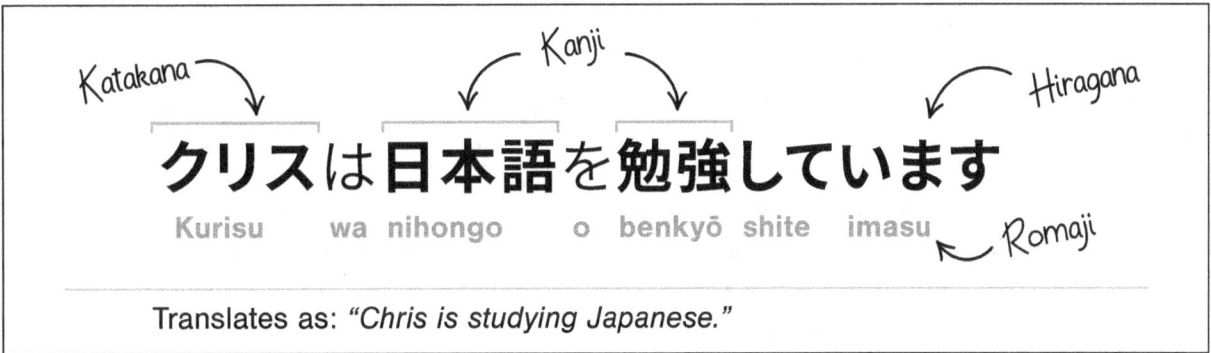

Translates as: *"Chris is studying Japanese."*

Romaji

Romaji is the **English lettering** used to transcribe Japanese symbols into a format that beginners can read and understand. It illustrates the sounds that make up the language when first starting, but it's not truly compatible with Japanese sounds, so often inaccurate. You will find that romaji transcriptions may also vary from one learning resource to another and inconsistencies like that inevitably lead to confusion later.

With very few practical uses beyond learning pronunciations, you should aim to reduce your reliance on romaji and eliminate it from your studies as soon as you can memorize the kana scripts. *After all, you aim to learn Japanese!*

Hiragana & Katakana

The subsequent two alphabets are known collectively as the **Kana scripts**, and they are distinctly *Japanese-looking* by comparison. Each consists of 46 basic characters (or *'letters'*) and they are used frequently throughout the language, often together.

Kana characters are very different from other alphabets. Technically, **Hiragana and Katakana** are **'phonetic syllabaries,'** meaning individual symbols represent a sound instead of a letter. It also means that each character is pronounced as a separate, distinct *'syllable'* when speaking Japanese. They are essential for kanji study *(the fourth character system)*.

Japanese writing typically contains characters from each of the hiragana, katakana, and kanji scripts, although we never mix hiragana and katakana within a single word. You will soon recognize which is which, but they are easy to tell apart when you look at the general shapes:

Hiragana tend to have more rounded shapes and are drawn or written with curved, sometimes sweeping, lines *(a little like cursive handwriting)*. Katakana generally have more angular or pointy shapes, by comparison:

The two sets of kana represent the same sounds, but each script has different uses within the language. Very briefly, hiragana is used to show how to pronounce kanji *(effectively spelling them out)* and also to show grammatical information. On the other hand, Katakana is used to spell words from outside Japan - *foreign vocabulary, such as names, objects, brands, etc., from overseas* - and for spelling your name. Later in the book, you will learn more about the different ways in which you can use both of the kana scripts.

Kanji

Japanese Kanji characters are *extremely numerous* compared to the kana, and there are tens of thousands in existence, with more created over time. To be considered literate in Japan, one must memorize over two thousand, but you can start reading lots of everyday Japanese with a knowledge of *just a few hundred*.

The kanji writing system is very different from the kana scripts, as the characters represent large blocks of meaning and vocabulary - for the most part, verbs and nouns. Essentially, they are the types of words that make up most of any language. Some of the characters are simple in appearance, even resembling the kana in some instances, but lots of kanji are far more complex-looking. Kanji are also combined to make additional words with new, often related meanings.

Initially adopted from the Chinese language, Japanese kanji often have more than one meaning, and most will usually have several different pronunciations. It's easy to see why Japanese is considered one of the most challenging languages to learn. The writing system works relatively logically, making it easier to study than you may think.

Writing in Japanese

In addition to helping with memorization, the careful writing of characters or texts is a part of learning Japanese. Both the way and order in which we draw lines can affect the shape and legibility of your writing. Before you begin learning about hiragana, the following pages provide some practical information about Japanese text and writing.

Text Direction

When Japan first imported the kanji writing system from China, it adopted the vertical writing configuration, show to the right *(A)*. Vertical text is written and read in columns, starting in the upper right, from top to bottom, and from right to left. The spine of all books, magazines, and newspapers with vertical text is positioned on the right side. *They are, effectively, read back to front compared to books written in English.*

Modern Japanese uses the more familiar horizontal writing direction *(B)*. Text is read and written in rows, from *left to right*, and top to bottom, as in European languages that use the Roman lettering system.

The text direction tends to be apparent from the line spacing, creating a gap for certain types of notation. *You can read more about this in a later chapter on kanji.*

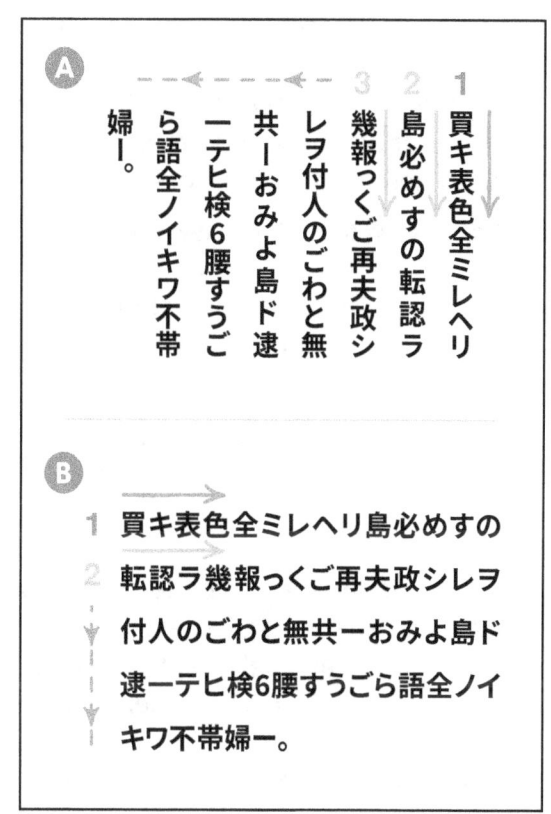

Above: the same dummy text in (A) vertical and (B) horizontal writing directions.

Stroke Order

The lines that make up Japanese characters are all drawn in a set order. You will learn the correct way to write individual kana and develop muscle memory through practice.

In most cases, two rules apply: we start in the upper left of a symbol, and make strokes from left to right, top to bottom until reaching the lower right.

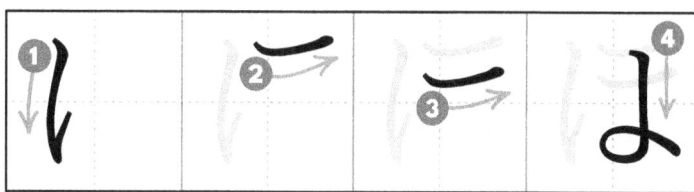

Some slightly extended rules apply to kanji, but the same general steps still apply.

Text Styles

Japanese characters can be presented in a wide variety of styles, from ornate, brushed calligraphy, to the contemporary, bold typefaces featured on packaging designs. While words and characters may have a completely different appearance from one place to another, they always mean the same thing.

Just as there is a wide range of fonts or typefaces available for *Roman* lettering, the style of Japanese symbols can be altered to suit different styles, tones, and designs. There are two types of system font at a basic level with slight but notable differences:

Serif fonts feature decorative flourishes and lines of varied thickness, replicating details found in handwritten characters:

- Similar style to: [**Times New Roman**]

Sans-serif or *Gothic* fonts are more uniform or *'plain,'* with consistent line thicknesses and no added decoration:

- Similar style to [**Century Gothic**]

Above: kanji 日本語 means "Japanese (language)"

Like any language, Japanese handwriting comes in all shapes and sizes, both tidy and... *less so*. As with any calligraphy, you can often see *how* characters have been written, and the more writing practice you do, the easier it becomes to recognize characters written by other people:

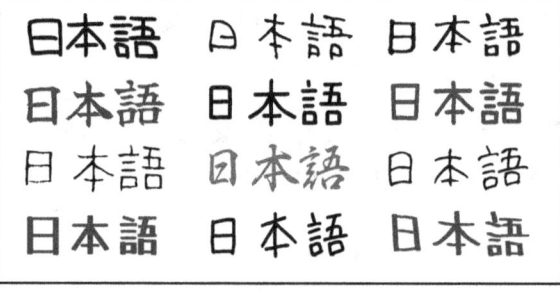

Bold and modern fonts provide lots of options for contemporary designs. Some can be pretty abstract, but most make for effective display typography. Decorative flourishes tend to be more for the style than they are for replicating handwriting. The characters that you know are easily understood, with shapes that are more well-defined:

Kana and kanji can look significantly different without losing their meaning, as long as their overall *proportion and shapes remain the same* relative to the other characters.

Stroke Types

There are three distinctly different types of mark that you can make with your pen. It may be tricky to emulate these shapes unless using a a brush-tipped pen and, in some ways, this style of writing is comparable with cursive handwriting, so not *essential*.

Referred to as a *'tome'* or *'stop stroke'*, from 止める (とめる), or *Tomeru*, which means "to stop", these lines have clearly defined start and end points. Your pen or pencil is brought to a hard stop before lifting from the page:

The second type of mark, known as a *'sweep'* or *'harai'*, comes from the Japanese 払う (はらう), or *Harau*, meaning "to sweep". It also features a well-defined start point but as you approach the end of the stroke, you would flick your pen from the paper. The line should continue in the same direction, slowly trailing off before lifting completely from the page:

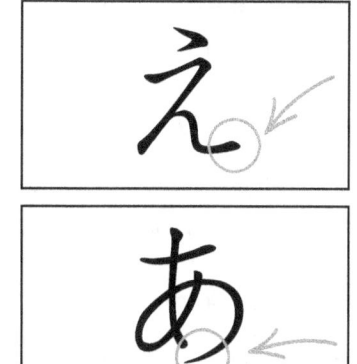

Typically referred to as a *'hane'*, from the Japanese 跳ねる (はねる), or *Haneru*, which means "to jump". These strokes are confident lines where your pen or pencil is flicked from the paper, usually in the opposite direction:

Most people use a ballpoint pen or pencil to write, making it difficult to achieve this level of accuracy. Unless you intend to practice more traditional styles of calligraphy, concentrate on the shape of your kana characters before addressing these details.

Writing in this Book

This workbook is for writing in, and while the paper is relatively good quality, you should try to avoid using any markers or pens with especially wet ink that is prone to bleeding. The pages are better suited to ballpoint pens, pencils, or even gel-based stationery, which should not transfer to the pages beneath. *You can test your writing tools in the spaces below, checking how they affect the following pages:*

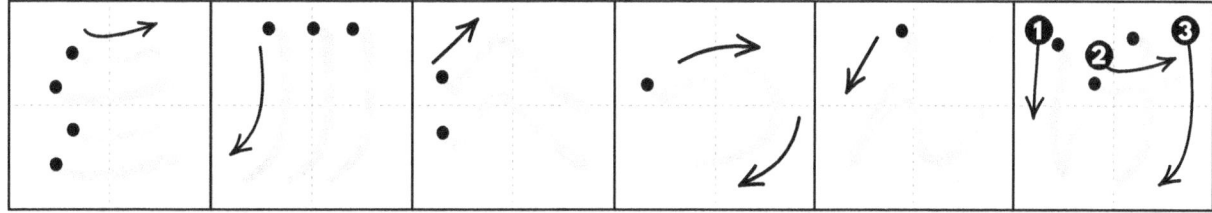

Once you have learned and practiced the kana, it could be worth investing in a notebook with a high-quality paper for advanced studies. A traditional brush-style pen can make your Japanese writing more natural-looking but require more specialist types of paper.

About Mnemonics

Mnemonics are simply tools that can aid with memorization. They are particularly effective for those learning Japanese, and we use them to remember what each of the characters represents.

Essentially, we can either associate new information with something we already know or develop a mechanism to prompt our brain to recall what we are learning. The kana scripts are visual representations of sounds, so we create mnemonics based on their shapes. An example may help to illustrate the point:

The hiragana あ represents an 'a-' or 'ah' sound. We transcribe it as equivalent to the letter 'a' in romaji, pronounced as a short 'ah,' similar to the 'a' in car, father, or apple.

It may be easier to remember if you visualize あ as having the shape of an apple *(also starting with the letter 'a')*. The shapes of the letters *'A'* and *'a'* also hide within the character あ. It doesn't matter how vague or obvious the connection, so long as it will remind you that あ = a / or an 'a- sound.'

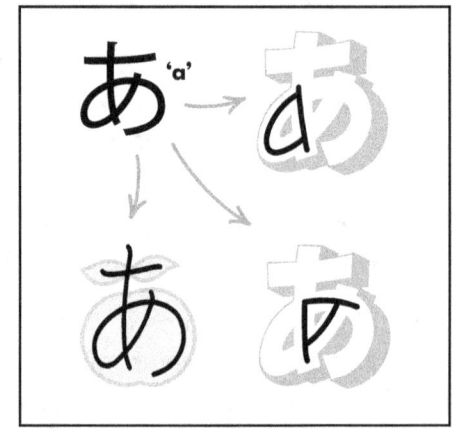

Examine the shape of each new symbol and the sound it represents. Look for any sort of immediate connections that can be made between the romaji version, the pronunciation, and its general appearance. You may need to think outside the box for some shapes, but even the most abstract ideas, once visualized a certain way, are not forgotten as quickly, and *that's the whole idea!*

Another example *(right)* shows a mnemonic created for the hiragana け *(or 'ke')*, pronounced in a similar way to the "ke-" in the word "keg." The character has a shape that looks a little like a barrel or *keg of beer*:

One of the more *obvious* mnemonics now, this time for the hiragana character の *(or 'no')*, which sounds and looks similar to the "no-" in the word "nose." This shape could be compared to a *'no smoking'* sign too:

Mnemonics may not work for everybody and can hamper progress for some learners. Some of the examples you find elsewhere will seem inaccurate or silly, putting people off their use. Try to come up with personal visualizations before dismissing them altogether. Even if you only recall a character from an especially bad mnemonic, it will have served its purpose and helped you to remember.

About 'Syllables'

Japanese is one of the few languages where pronunciation is based on timing and rhythm. We structure sounds around a system of **'mora,'** which are simply timing units in the context of language and speech. For ease, you can think of **'morae'** *(the plural of 'mora')* as *beats.* A *'moraic system'* organizes sound units differently to languages based on syllables, such as English.

Each kana character represents one syllable sound, and they all take one *mora*, or one *beat*, to pronounce. Words written with two kana take twice as much time to pronounce as one kana*, and those with three or four kana are three or four beats long. The actual amount of time is unimportant and will vary from one person to another, depending on how fast they talk.

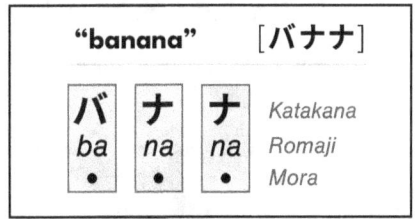

Above: 3 Syllable Word, 3 Mora.

If you're wondering the difference between a syllable and a mora, **syllables** are broad chunks of sound that can be of different lengths. Each has a vowel in the middle and consonants on one or both sides. **Morae** are smaller, timed units of sound that set an underlying rhythm by which we pronounce all Japanese sounds.

In the example (*right*), the kana have separate sounds that we say over two distinct beats in the Japanese pronunciation. The English pronunciation has just one syllable because the 'n,' without a vowel, attaches to the 'ka-' sound. Syllables in Japanese can contain multiple morae, but mora can have only one syllable sound:

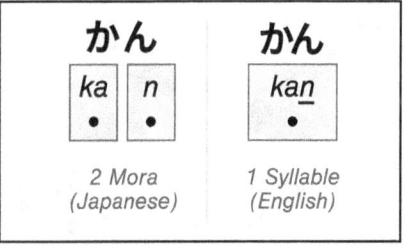

To further illustrate the difference: the Japanese word for 'teacher' is 先生, or 'Sensei.' This is a word that's also used in the English language to describe martial arts teachers. There are two units of sound *(two syllables)* in the English pronunciation, "sen-say." We spell the kanji 'reading' (pronunciation) using four hiragana, so it's four morae long and said in 4 equal beats. *Morae are the way that we differentiate between long and short syllables:*

We still speak Japanese in syllables, but morae dictate the timing with which each sound is made. We pronounce individual sounds at a fixed rate (at regular intervals), all roughly equal length. Hopefully, that should make some sense, but it may take some time and practice with the language to fully understand how mora work.

* Two characters are not *always* pronounced as two morae, but you will learn more about special *'combination kana'* and their sounds in a later chapter.

//////////////////////////////// **PART 2**

Hiragana

In some ways, hiragana is the most crucial alphabet to learn. Firstly, hiragana represent every sound that you need to speak Japanese. It's also an essential tool for further study, as we use it to read all of the kanji, effectively 'spelling' kanji words out with sounds.

Eventually, you will use hiragana across the whole writing system as they are suffixed to kanji *(Japanese words),* like verbs and adjectives, to provide extra information. Later still, you will use hiragana as *particles* to add structure to sentences and implement grammar. Before looking at any of those topics, the most important thing you can do is learn the alphabet.

As you work your way through this chapter, pay particular attention to how characters are pronounced. The *'alphabet'* in the following chapter represents the same sounds. Doing a thorough job here could save lots of time later.

The chart to the right shows all of the **46 basic hiragana symbols** you are about to learn. You should see that romaji vowels are written to one side, with consonant letters above, and most symbols follow a consistent pattern where two sounds are combined - we take a consonant (top row) and add a vowel sound afterward (right column), with just one exception.

This pattern will become your key to mastering the pronunciation of most hiragana. The basic vowel sounds in the right column are carried across the chart, with subsequent consonant sounds added in front to pronounce the others characters. All characters in the 'A-row' will sound similar, *e.g. ka, sa, ta, etc.*

Traditional Japanese texts are written and read from top to bottom, and from right to left, column by column. This chart should be read the same way but, in reality, you will find everyday modern Japanese texts are written from left to right - just like in English and other European languages.

Over the following pages, you will learn the alphabet in groups, roughly column by column. Learning the letters in chunks will make it more manageable. Each block of letters ends with a revision section to test your memory and determine where you might need more practice.

Notes:

* ん iis the only character in this table that we pronounce as a syllable without adding any of the vowel sounds.

** を is a *"particle"* and is used for grammar. We write it as *"wo"*, but it is transcribed in romaji as either *"o"* or *"wo"*.

Hiragana

	a	i	u	e	o	
	あ a	い i	う u	え e	お o	p. 022
k	か ka	き ki	く ku	け ke	こ ko	p. 030
s	さ sa	し shi	す su	せ se	そ so	p. 038
t	た ta	ち chi	つ tsu	て te	と to	p. 046
n	な na	に ni	ぬ nu	ね ne	の no	p. 055
h	は ha	ひ hi	ふ fu	へ he	ほ ho	p. 061
m	ま ma	み mi	む mu	め me	も mo	p. 069
y	や ya		ゆ yu		よ yo	p. 075
r	ら ra	り ri	る ru	れ re	ろ ro	p. 081
w	わ wa		ん *n		を **wo	p. 087

021

H1. The Vowel Column

The first column of the basic hiragana chart is arguably the most important. Learning how to pronounce all five characters in this group properly is going to make the rest much easier. They set you up with sounds that are used across the whole alphabet so it is worth spending time to practice these well.

Symbols in this learning block.

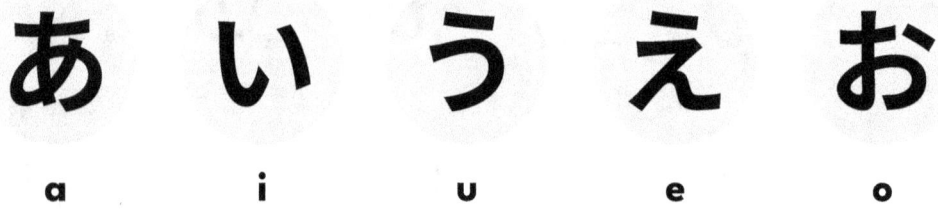

Pronunciation

Each of the vowel characters have a short, sharp pronunciation and these sounds should not be drawn out or elongated. The first symbol あ is pronounced as a short *'ah'* sound (like the *'a'* in *'apple'*) and not as *'ahh'*.

The second symbol い is shown in romaji as *'i'* but never pronounced like *'I'* (or, eye). It always has a shortened 'ee' sound, similar to the *'i'* in *'igloo'*.

When you pronounce the 'oo' sound for the third character, 'u' or う, your lips make a round shape and move forwards - try saying the word 'pool' once or twice. This is less pronounced with the Japanese *'u'* sound, and the *'oo'* sound is shorter.

The sound for the character え or *'e'* is similar to normal pronunciation in the middle of a word. It is a short *'eh'* sound, *like the 'e' in bed, tell, send, and so on.*

Lastly, お is the Japanese vowel sound for *'o'* and it is pronounced as *'oh'*, *like the 'o' in 'no' or 'original'*.

Similar to the 'a' sound in car, like 'ah'.

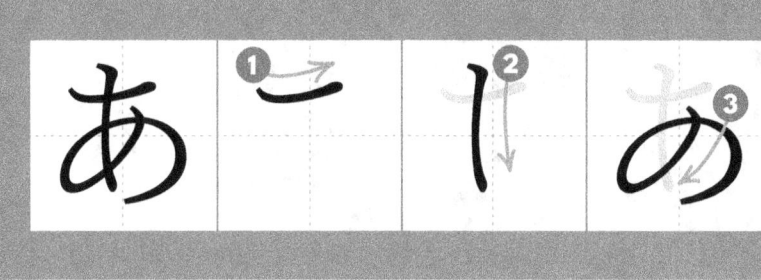

Practice writing あ by tracing these characters, using **three** strokes.

Try to maintain accurate shapes while writing あ on a smaller scale.

Mnemonic.

Examples.
- Shape of an <u>a</u>pple
- Contains letter 'a'

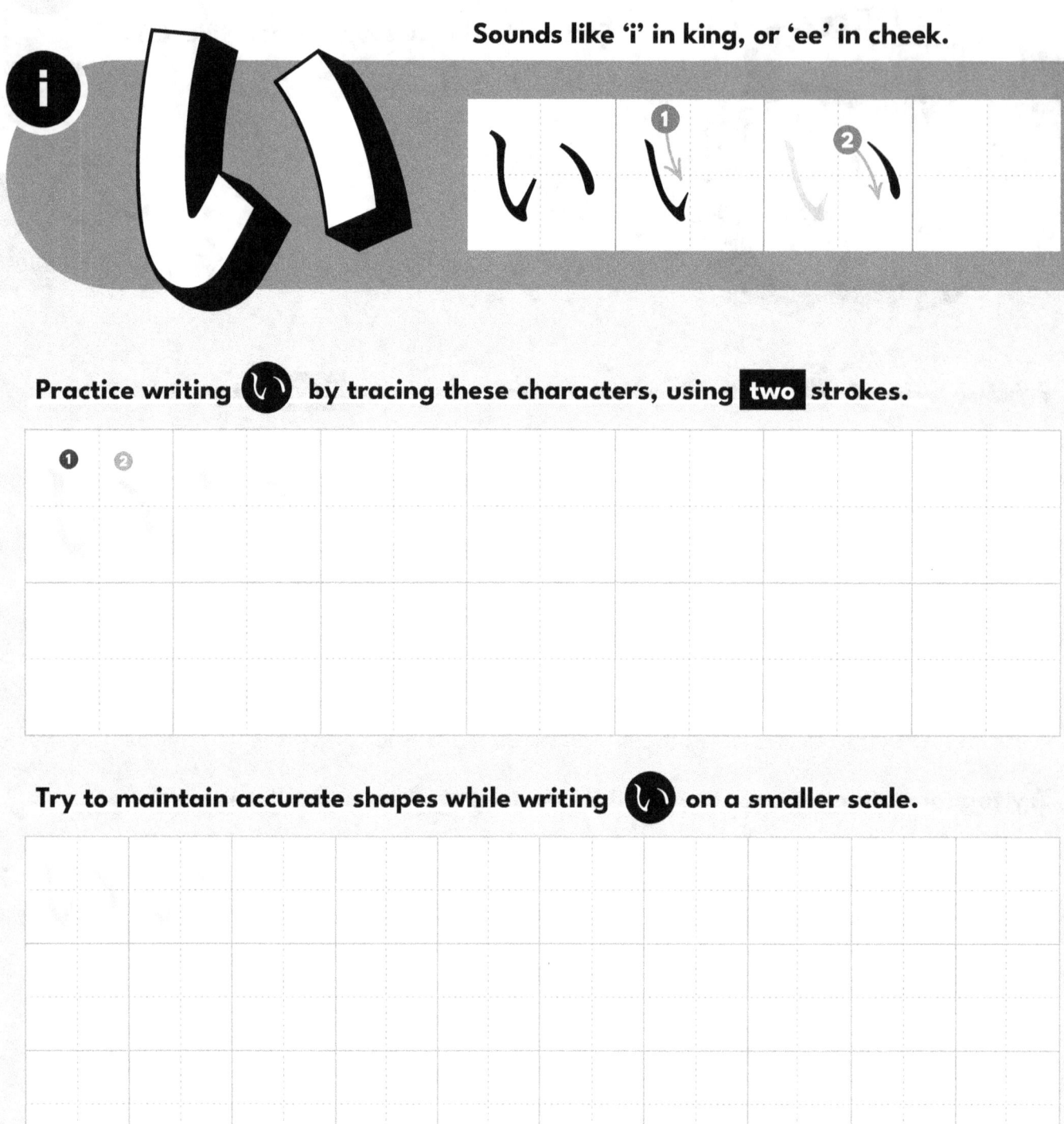

い

Sounds like 'i' in king, or 'ee' in cheek.

Practice writing い **by tracing these characters, using** two **strokes.**

Try to maintain accurate shapes while writing い **on a smaller scale.**

Mnemonic.

Examples.

- Letter 'i' x 2
- Picture two feet
- Pair of eels

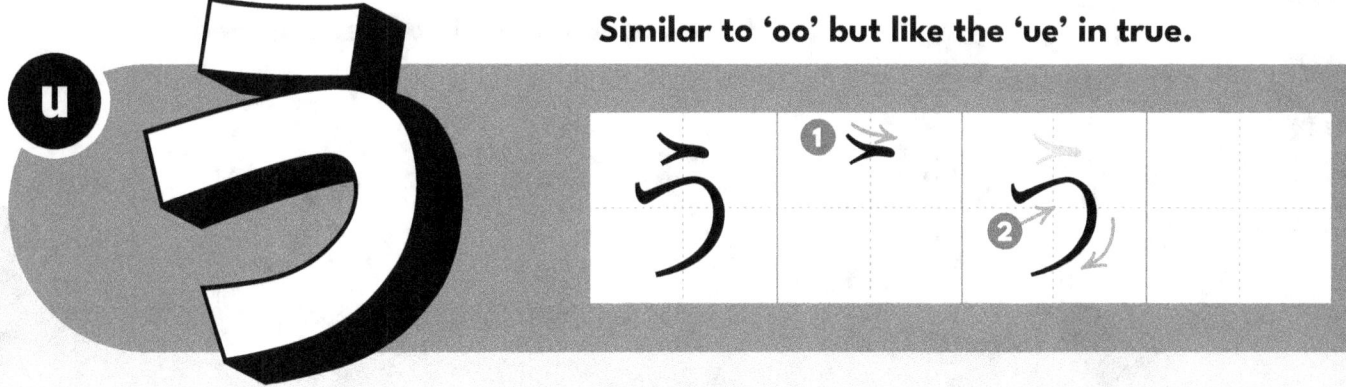

Similar to 'oo' but like the 'ue' in true.

Practice writing う by tracing these characters, using two strokes.

Try to maintain accurate shapes while writing う on a smaller scale.

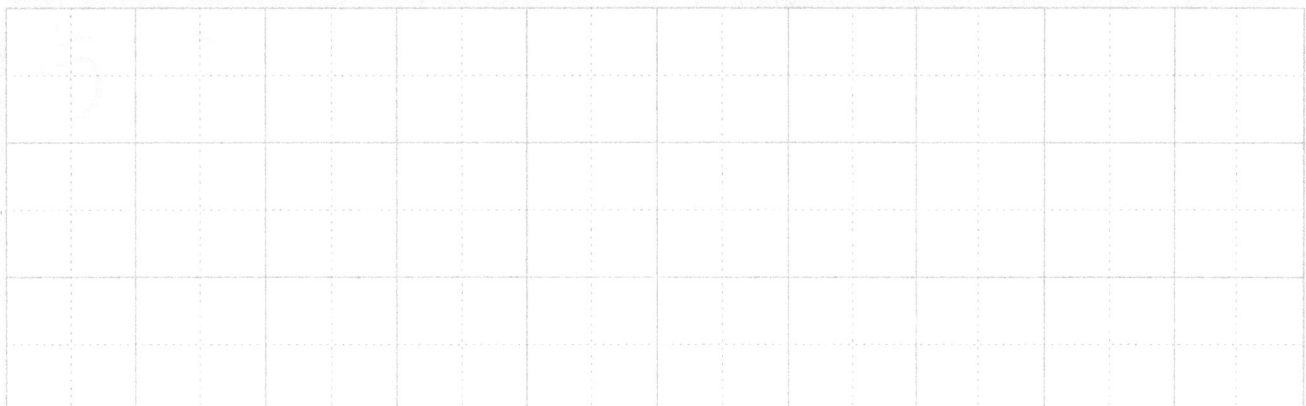

Mnemonic.

Examples.
- Sideways letter 'u'
- Imagine an open mouth eating f<u>oo</u>d

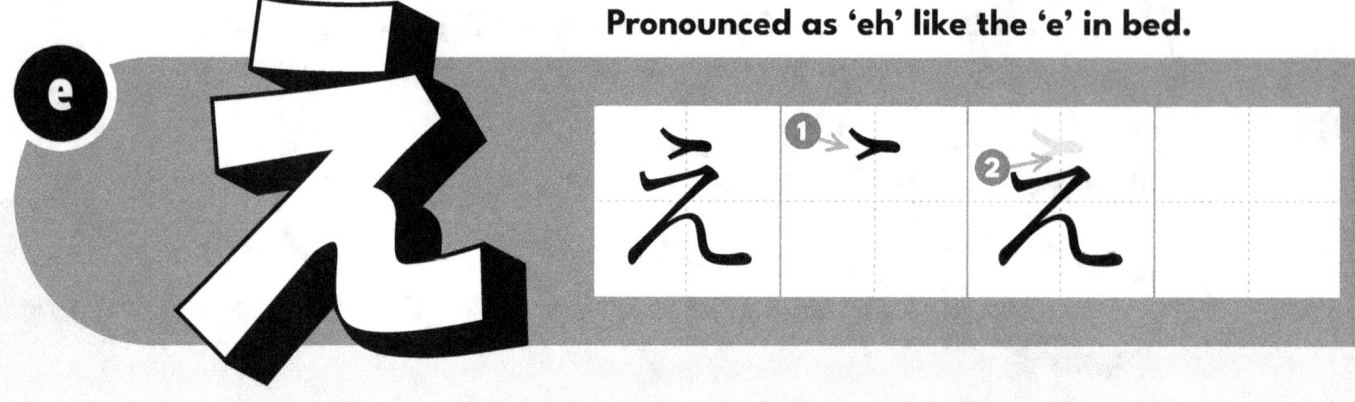

Pronounced as 'eh' like the 'e' in bed.

Practice writing え by tracing these characters, using two strokes.

Try to maintain accurate shapes while writing え on a smaller scale.

Mnemonic.

Examples & ideas.

- Looks energetic, like a running man
- Shape of exotic bird

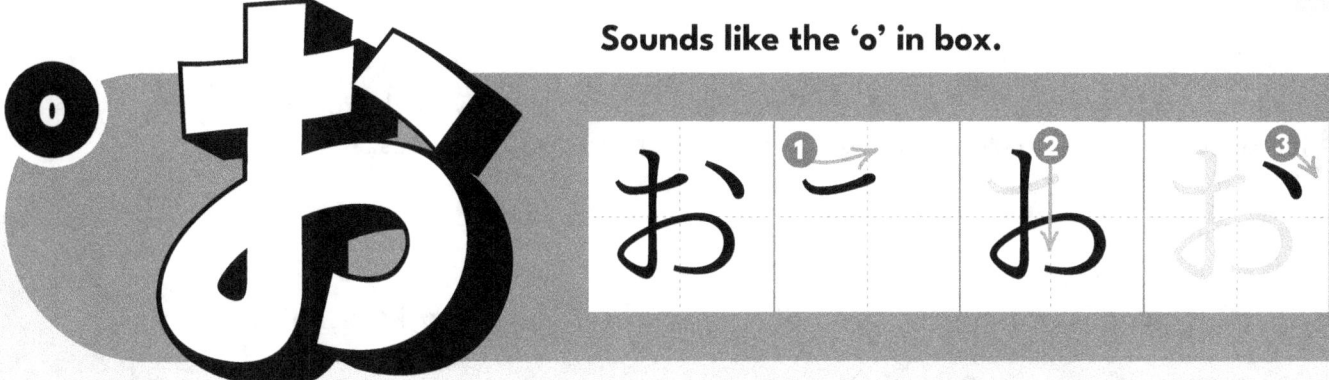

Sounds like the 'o' in box.

Practice writing お by tracing these characters, using three strokes.

Try to maintain accurate shapes while writing お on a smaller scale.

Mnemonic.

Examples.
- Picture an <u>O</u>live <u>o</u>n a stick
- Contains letter 'o'

How good is your memory? This exercise should be easy but try to write the romaji for each of these hiragana in the boxes below - without looking back at the previous pages.

Practice pronouncing each symbol as you write the romaji beneath.

あ い う え お あ い お う あ え あ う あ

え お あ い う え お い あ え お い う え

い う あ え お え う あ お あ う い お あ

Take a break for 5 minutes, and then do the same for these symbols too.

う い う あ え い え い お い あ お え う

い え う あ お う お え い お え う あ い

あ い え あ い え あ う い あ え あ い お

Reading Practice

With the ability to recognize the sounds that each character represents, you can start to read Japanese words. Reading is a great way to practice the language and simultaneously collect new vocabulary. You should try to practice your pronunciation at the same time by reading aloud.

When we read Japanese words, each *'syllable sound'* should take the same length of time to say. When we write characters together to form words, we pronounce each character one after the other - the sounds are not usually* merged. For example, the term **あい** *(meaning love)* is pronounced as *'a-i'* so that both sounds can be heard *("ah-ee")*.

The pronunciation of vowels like *'a'* and *'i'* often changes when they are joined together in English words. Compare how you pronounce the word *"man"* to the word *"main"* or how the vowels sound when you say *"bit,"* *"bat,"* and *"bait."* Some describe Japanese as more straightforward to learn as a foreign language than English because what you see is often what you say.

We can write several words using just those five hiragana you have learned so far. Some examples are shown below, with space to write the romaji for each:

あう		to meet	あい		love/ indigo
いえ		house	あお		blue
おい		nephew	ああ		ah! / oh!
うえ		up/above	いい		good
いう		to say	おう		chase/King

* Certain letter combinations can be written and pronounced differently. You will learn more about these later in this book.

H2. The K Column

The second column of the chart has similar pronunciation to the vowel column. All that is needed to pronounce these characters is a *'k-'* sound in front of the vowel sounds. In other words, the *'eh'* sound of え becomes a *'keh'* sound, and so on.

Symbols in this learning block.

Pronunciation

The *'k-'* sound that you add to each of the vowel sounds is made in much the same way as in English. Your tongue is pressed up into the upper part of the mouth, towards the back of your mouth.

This is a *'voiceless'* consonant sound, meaning that your vocal chords are not used when you say it out loud. The sound is made as you push air through them and out of your mouth. These types of sounds have relatively high levels of aspiration when pronounced by an English speaker.

Aspiration is just the name for the force that is applied to air being pushed out of your mouth. You can feel the level of aspiration your normal *'k-'* sound has by holding your hand in front of your mouth and saying words like *'key'* or *'kelp'*. The real Japanese *'k-'* sound is not as strong, so try to hold back some of that force as you pronounce the sounds.

Pronounce like the 'kha' in khakis.

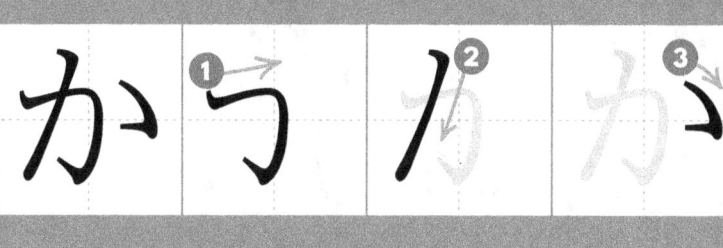

Practice writing か by tracing these characters, using three strokes.

Try to maintain accurate shapes while writing か on a smaller scale.

Mnemonic.

Examples.
- Letter 'k' shape with piece broken off
- Picture kicking a <u>ca</u>n up in the air.

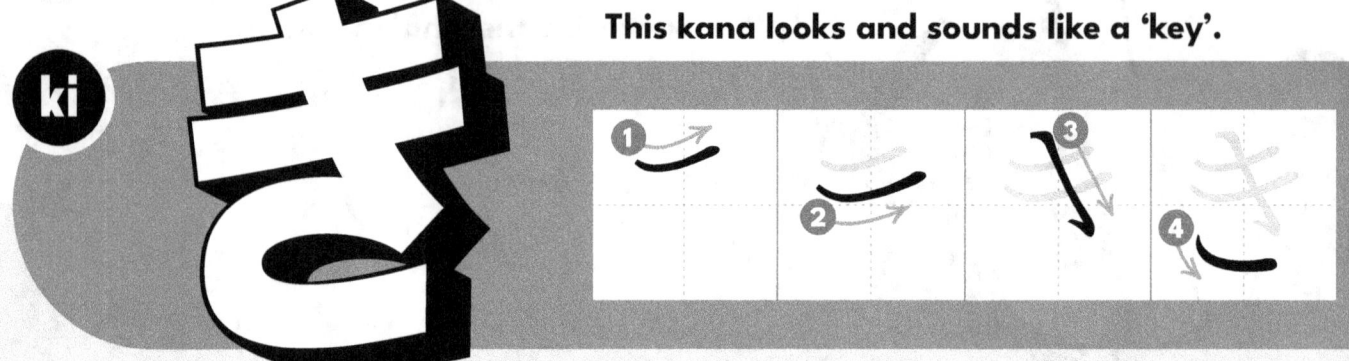

This kana looks and sounds like a 'key'.

Practice writing ぎ the correct way, with four* strokes (not three).

Try to maintain accurate shapes while writing ぎ on a smaller scale.

Mnemonic.

Examples.

- Looks like a key, for the '<u>ki</u>' sound

ku

Pronounced like the 'coo' in cool.

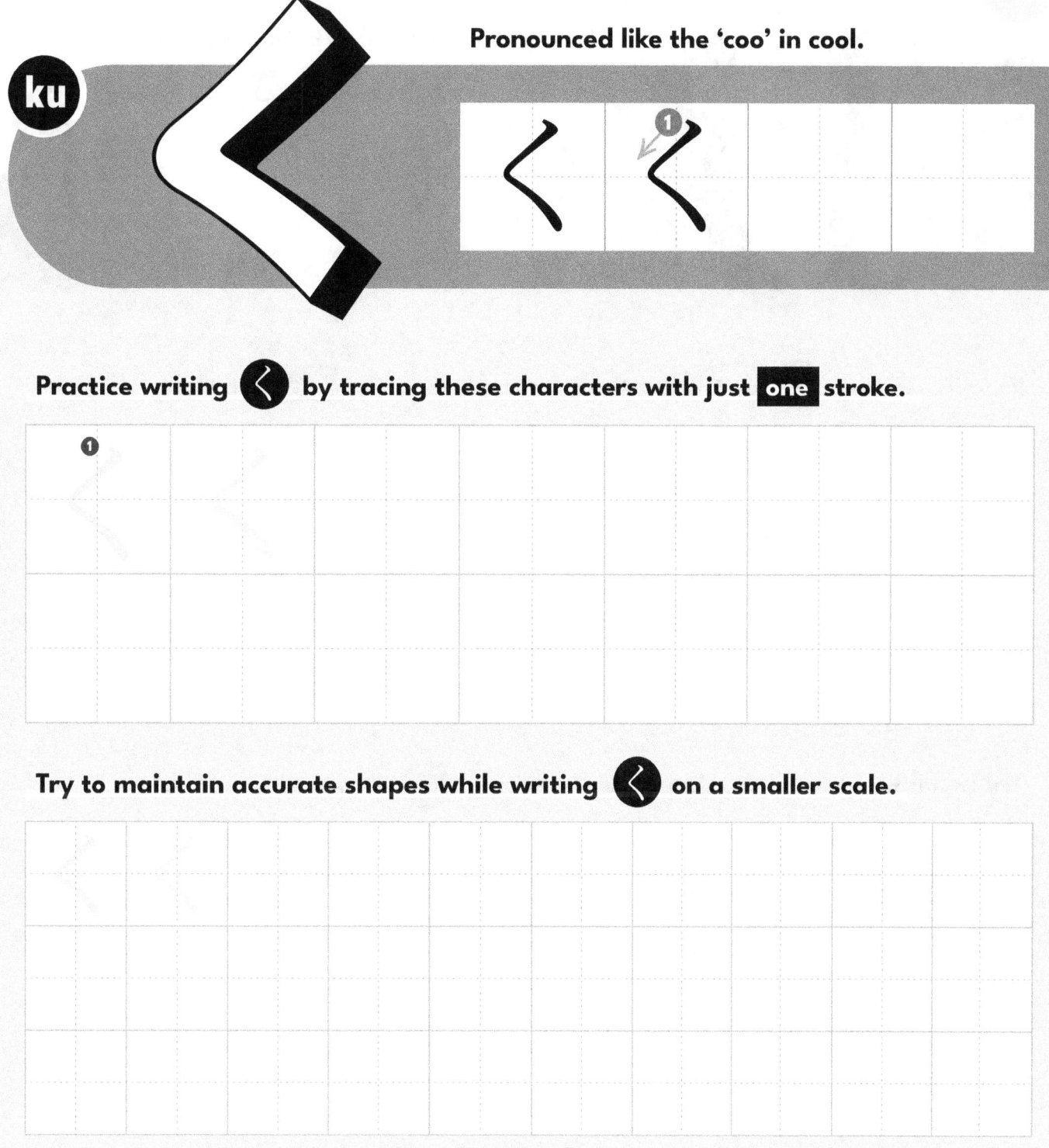

Practice writing く by tracing these characters with just one stroke.

Try to maintain accurate shapes while writing く on a smaller scale.

Mnemonic.

Examples.
- Picture the beak of a cuckoo bird.
- Or any coo-ing bird

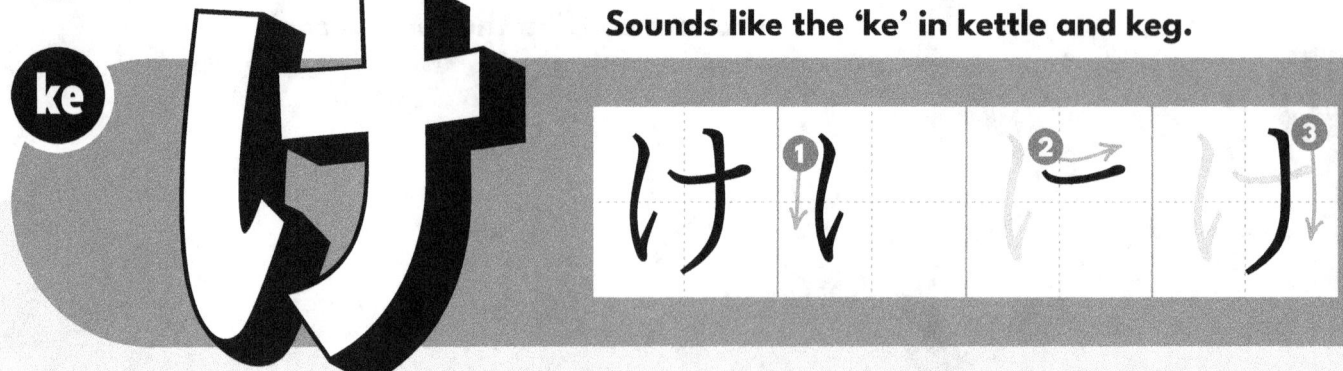

Sounds like the 'ke' in kettle and keg.

Practice writing け by tracing these characters, using three strokes.

Try to maintain accurate shapes while writing け on a smaller scale.

Mnemonic.

Examples.

- Picture as a barrel shape, or <u>keg</u>
- Could be a broken <u>kettle</u>

ko

Sounds like the 'co' in comb.

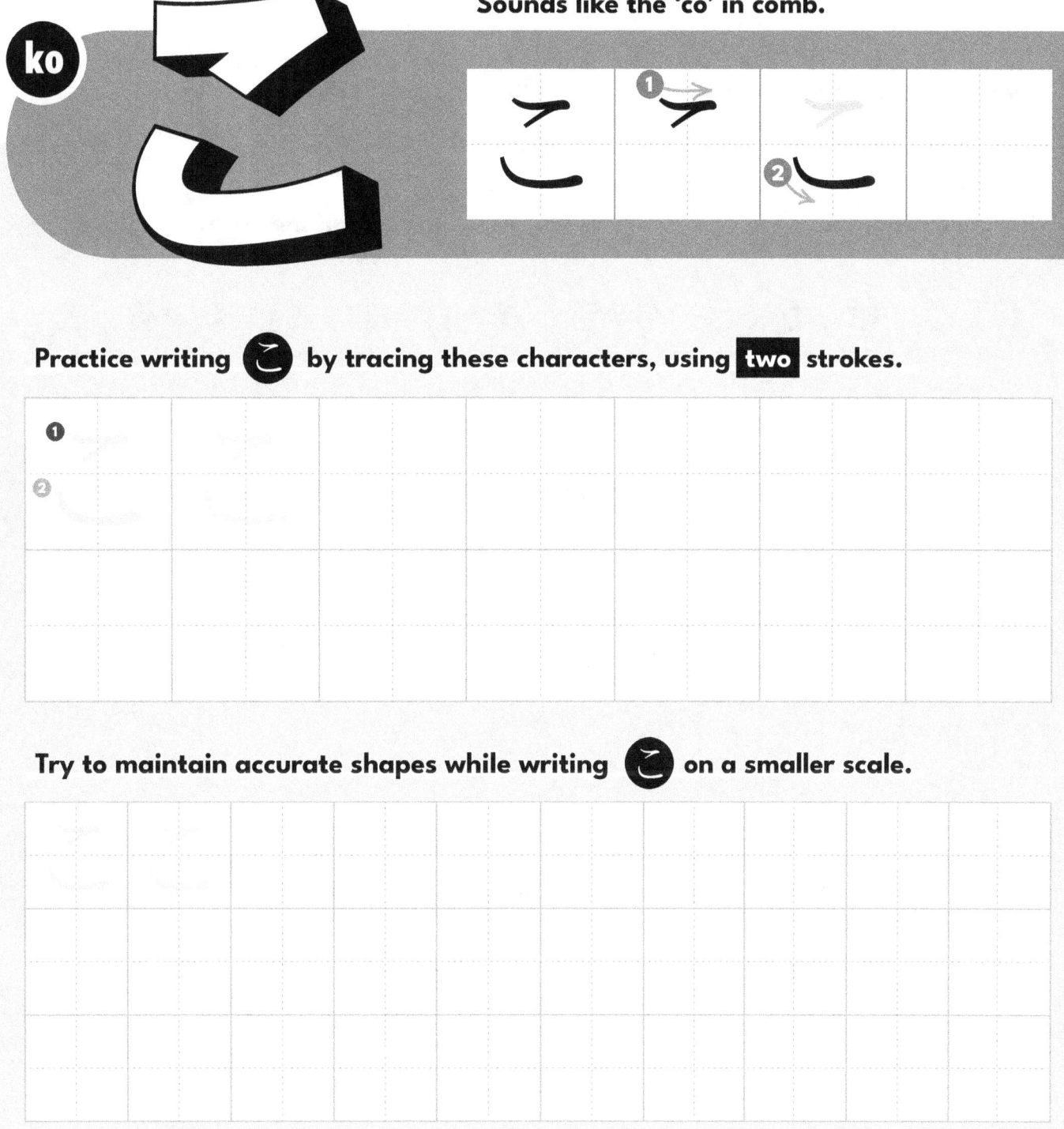

Practice writing こ by tracing these characters, using **two** strokes.

Try to maintain accurate shapes while writing こ on a smaller scale.

Mnemonic.

Examples.
- Could resemble a round <u>co</u>in shape
- Maybe a <u>co</u>rner?
- Rolling can of <u>co</u>la?

This set of exercises should be more challenging than the previous set, as it includes all ten of the hiragana you have learned. Once again, write the romaji for the characters below.

Practice pronouncing each symbol as you write the romaji beneath.

え う け か う く き か け お い く あ こ

え こ か お け こ お え く か け あ こ お

く き い お か く こ あ き い け き け き

Take a 5-minute break, and then do the same for this set of symbols too.

き か け お え こ け い か く き い え く

く け お か こ お く か お あ き お く う

い こ う こ け お え き く か き あ こ け

Practice reading and writing words with characters from all group so far.

あい
love

あう
meet

うえ
above / top

こえ
voice

お
hill

かく
write

きく
hear / ask

おけ
wooden bucket

こけ
moss

かお
face / honor

いけ
pond

あき
autumn

かう
buy

いう
say

えき
station

あかい
red

いく
go

あおい
blue

 here
ここ

きおく
memory

H3. The S Column

The *[consonant + vowel]* pattern applies to most groups of symbols, but not all. This third group contains the first of a few exceptions you will meet along the way. Fortunately, they are not any more difficult to pronounce.

Symbols in this learning block.

Pronunciation

With the exception of the second character, the symbols in this column follow the usual pattern. Simply add a normal *'s-'* sound to the vowels you have learned.

The exception here is し or *'shi'* which is pronounced slightly differently. Instead of saying *'si' (like 'see')* this character is *'shi'* and sounds like the English word *'she'*.

Accurate pronunciation of a Japanese 'sh-' is not far from the English 'sh' and it is unlikely to cause problems. If you want to achieve a more accurate sound, the tongue would need to make a slightly different shape. You may be able to feel the difference by saying the words *'he'* and *'she'* alternately a few times. The tongue tends to be pushed upwards with a bend in the middle when you say *'he'*. Introduce more of this tongue shape into your pronunciation of *'shi'*.

Sounds like the 'sa-' in sarcasm.

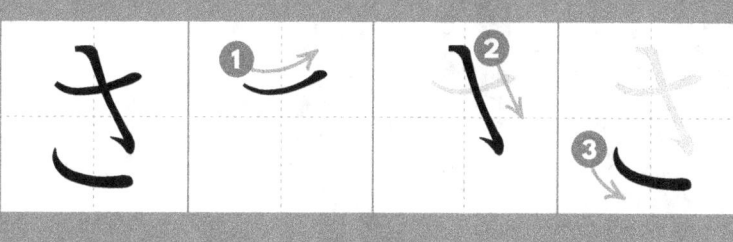

Practice writing さ the proper way, with **three*** strokes (not two).

Try to maintain accurate shapes while writing さ on a smaller scale.

Mnemonic.

Examples.
- Imagine the shapes as a <u>sa</u>d face?
- Similar to KI, but not the <u>sa</u>me

040

shi

Sounds exactly like the 'shi' in sashimi.

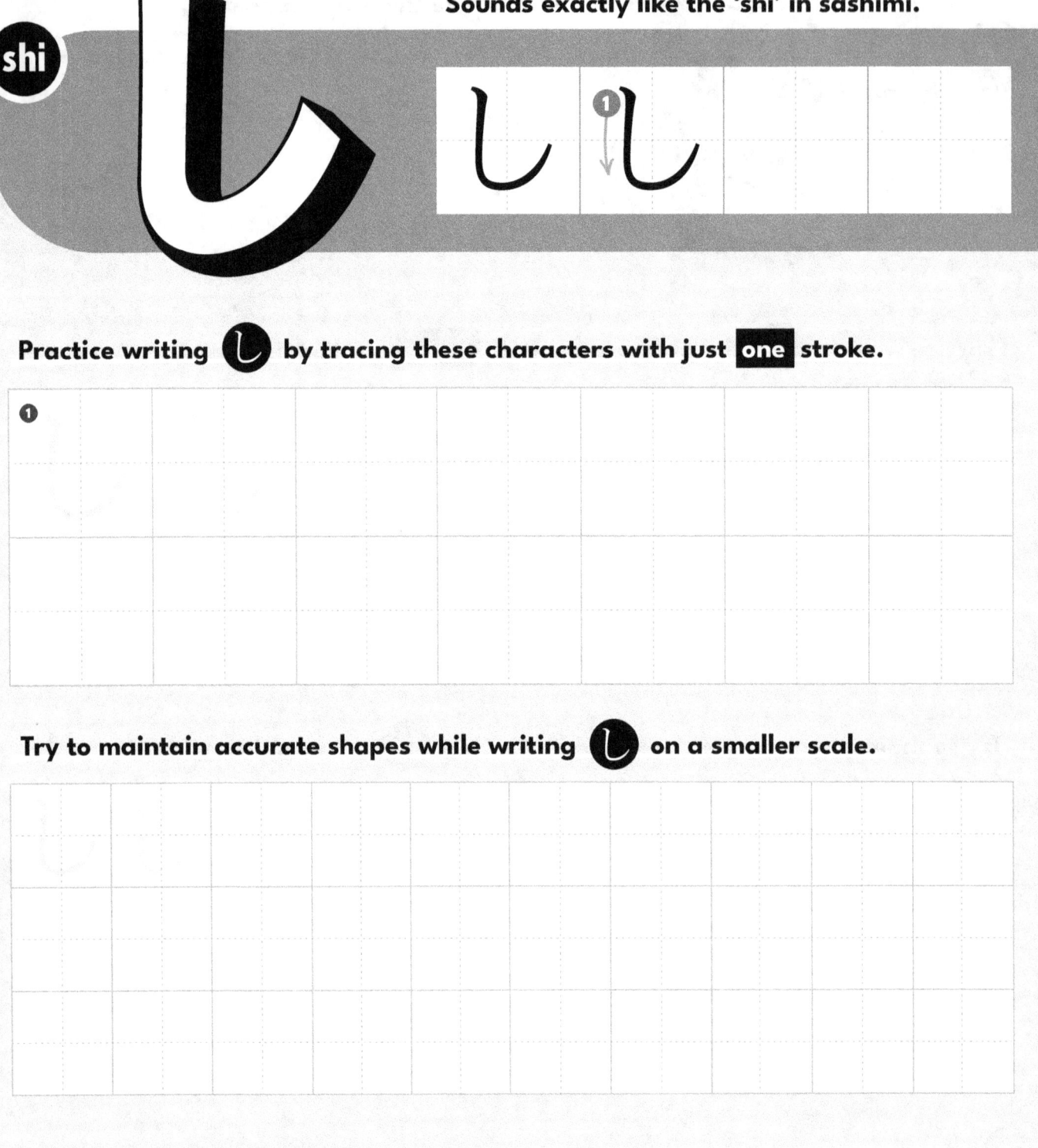

Practice writing し by tracing these characters with just **one** stroke.

Try to maintain accurate shapes while writing し on a smaller scale.

Mnemonic.

Examples.
- A **<u>fi</u>shing** hook
- <u>She</u> has long hair

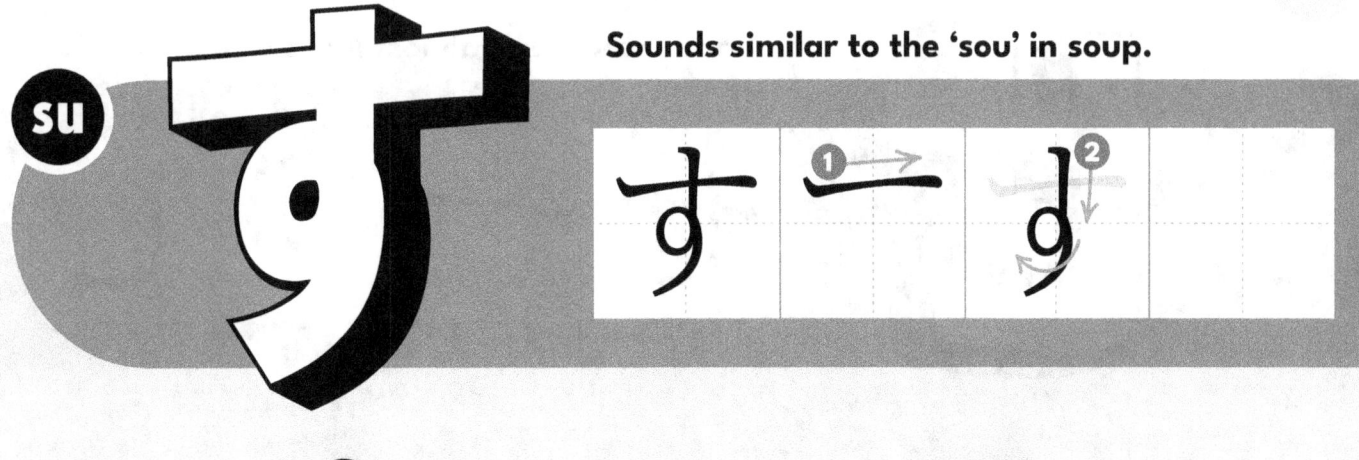

Sounds similar to the 'sou' in soup.

Practice writing す by tracing these characters, using **two** strokes.

Try to maintain accurate shapes while writing す on a smaller scale.

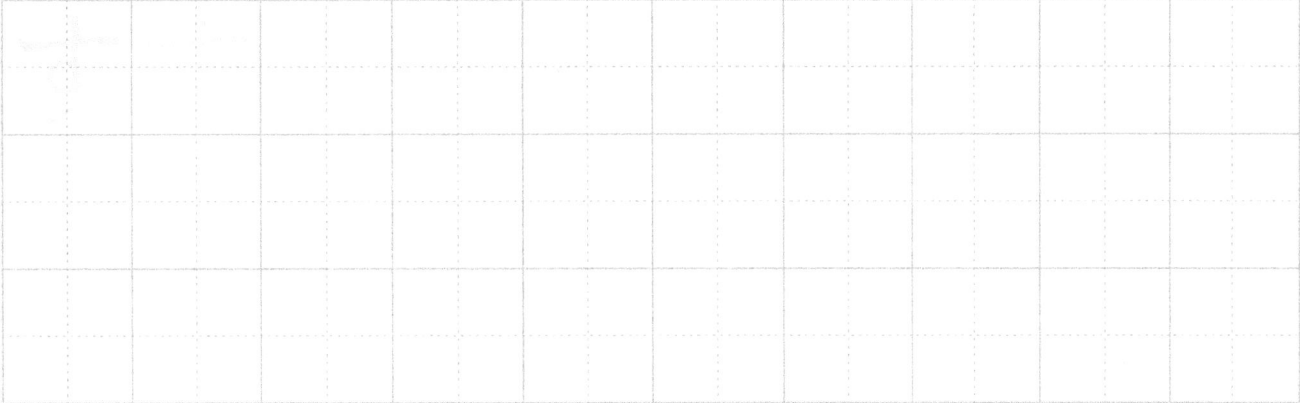

Mnemonic.

Examples.
- Picture a pig with a curly tail, called <u>Sue</u>
- Somebody wearing a hat, oh it's <u>Sue</u>

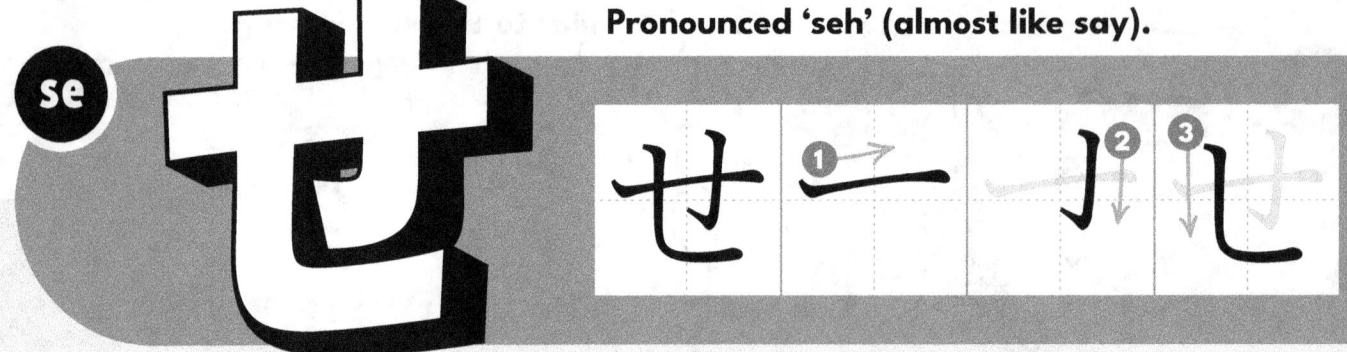

Pronounced 'seh' (almost like say).

Practice writing せ by tracing these characters, using three strokes.

Try to maintain accurate shapes while writing せ on a smaller scale.

Mnemonic.

Examples.
- imagine its a mouth <u>seh</u>-ing something
- Upside down <u>seven</u>s

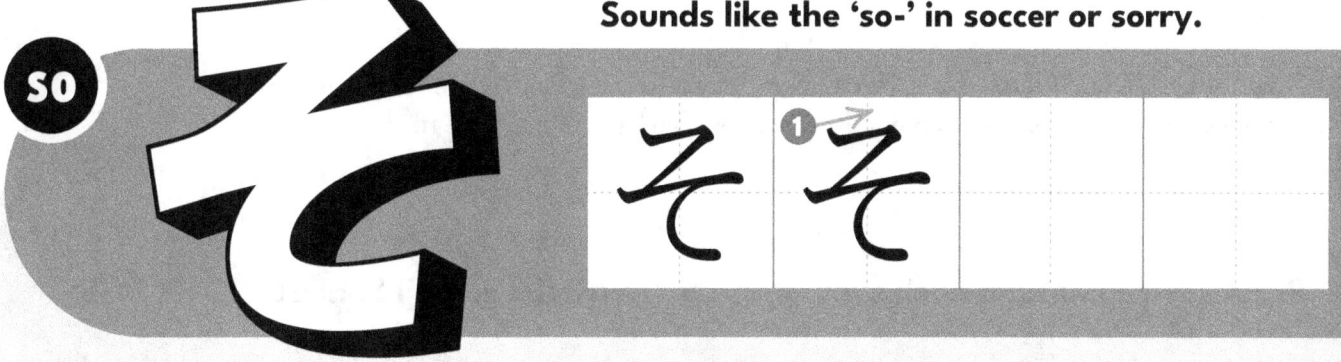

SO そ

Sounds like the 'so-' in soccer or sorry.

Practice writing そ **by tracing these characters with just one stroke.**

Try to maintain accurate shapes while writing そ **on a smaller scale.**

Mnemonic.

Examples.
- It's <u>so</u> abstract
- Picture a <u>sewing</u> needle and thread

Now that the five new hiragana have been added to the others, repeat this memorization exercise. Take a break between each set, as this will help to improve recall.

Practice pronouncing each symbol as you write the romaji beneath.

そ し す そ さ そ こ い え か せ お し そ

せ さ せ き す う し く さ す か う す き

こ あ か け き け そ い せ こ し す さ せ

Take a 5-minute break, and then do the same for these symbols too.

か き い す そ せ さ く き け そ さ お せ

さ か こ し あ せ こ し う す さ そ せ し

か け す き う せ し す す そ せ え い こ

This time, take a 10-minute break and come back to complete these.

き す く し す さ か そ せ か う せ そ さ

す し か せ こ そ さ お き き す せ え い

あ さ け い う こ こ け し そ そ せ し す

After a much longer break, add the romaji for each symbol below.

せ そ あ す お く き そ さ し か こ け う

き う す せ け そ さ え す こ そ こ か お

く し そ す か い き せ さ す せ い し そ

H4. The T-Column

The fourth column contains two characters that fall outside the usual pattern but, once again, they are not difficult to say and simply need to be remembered. They only really seem like exceptions because of the romaji beneath and, before long, you will simply recognize the character as the sound that it represents.

Symbols in this learning block.

Pronunciation

Characters with the pure *'t-'* sound are simple enough to pronounce. The tip of your tongue touches the top of your mouth, just behind your upper teeth, and air is released with some aspiration. Try to reduce the amount of force and air that is released.

The second character in the T column is simply pronounced as *'chi'* or a short *'chee-'*. While not exactly the same as the *'ch-'* in English pronunciation, this will be close enough. To achieve a more accurate pronunciation, the tip of your tongue would make contact with the roof of your mouth still, but further back from the position for a pure *'t-'* sound. It would be located on the area that feels slightly ribbed, at the end of the ridge that runs across the roof of your mouth, from front to back.

Finally, the character つ represents a *'tsu'* sound. The *'u'* part of the sound is the same as the basic vowel character う but the *'t-'* sound is now a *'ts-'*. Try not to view this as a silent *'t'*, as it should certainly be heard. Instead, try to isolate the sound of *'-ts'* from words like *'boats'* or *'knots'* and add the short *'oo'* sound to that. This almost sounds like the word *'zoo'* but shorter and with the *'t'*. Remember that this syllable is no longer than the others and is pronounced in the same length of time.

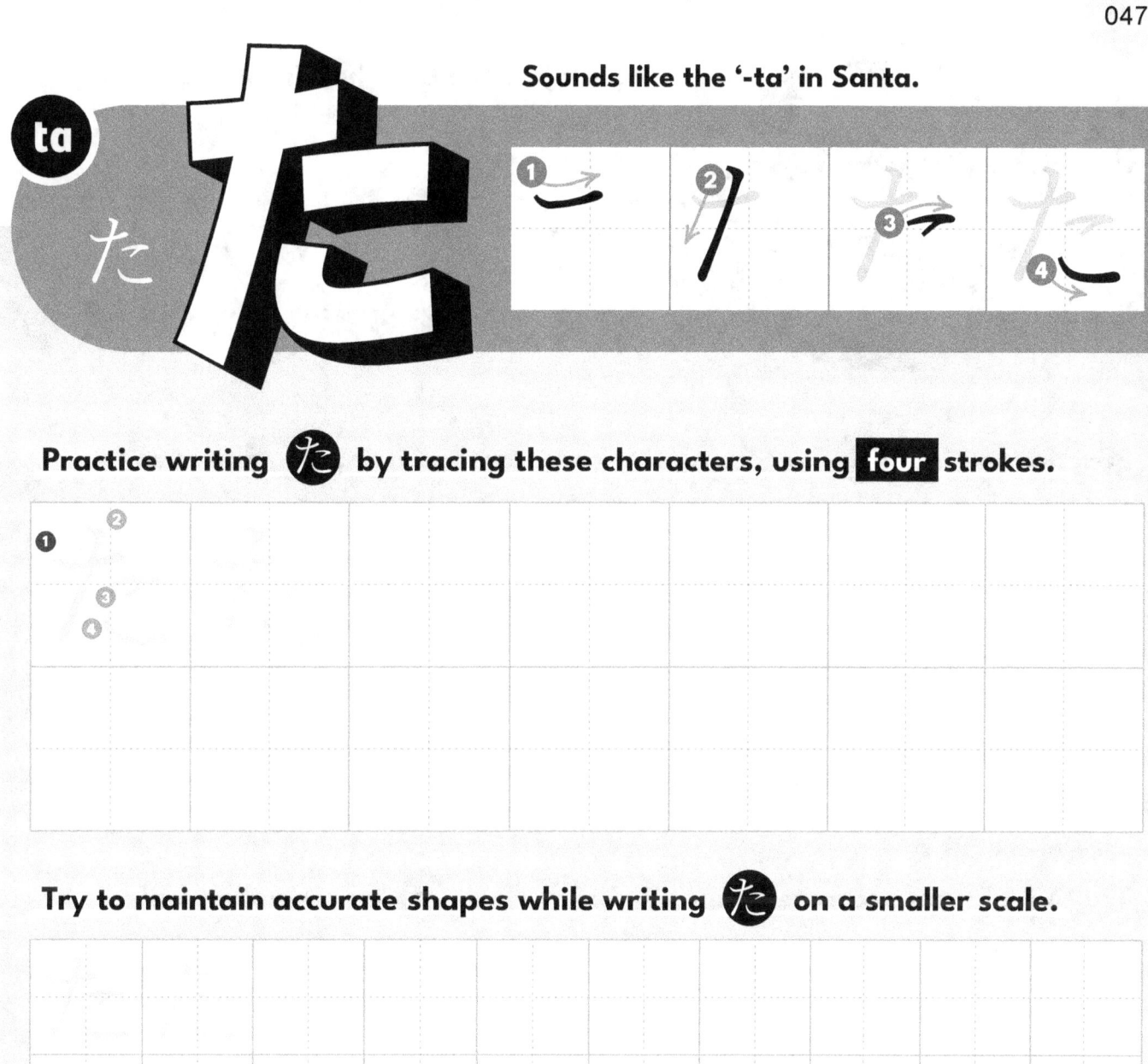

Sounds like the '-ta' in Santa.

Practice writing た by tracing these characters, using **four** strokes.

Try to maintain accurate shapes while writing た on a smaller scale.

Mnemonic.

Examples.
- Looks like letters 'ta'
- Tackling a ball

chi

Sounds just like the 'chee' in cheeks.

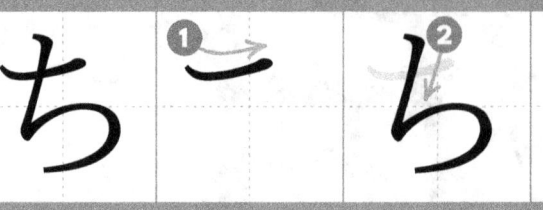

Practice writing ち by tracing these characters, using two strokes.

Try to maintain accurate shapes while writing ち on a smaller scale.

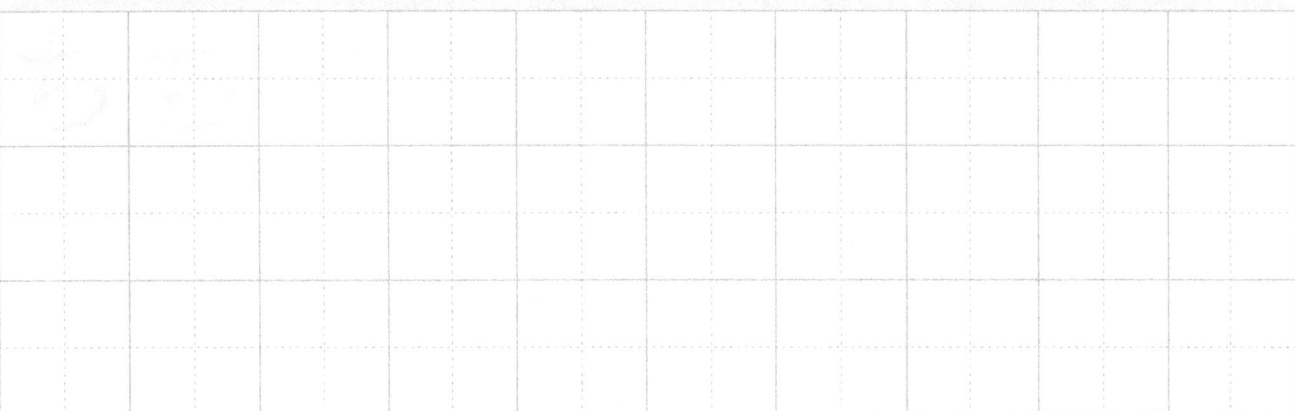

Mnemonic.

Examples.

- A face, from the side with no <u>ch</u>in
- It sneezes, Aa<u>chi</u>oo!
- A <u>ch</u>eap number 5?

tsu

Sounds just like the name 'Sue'.

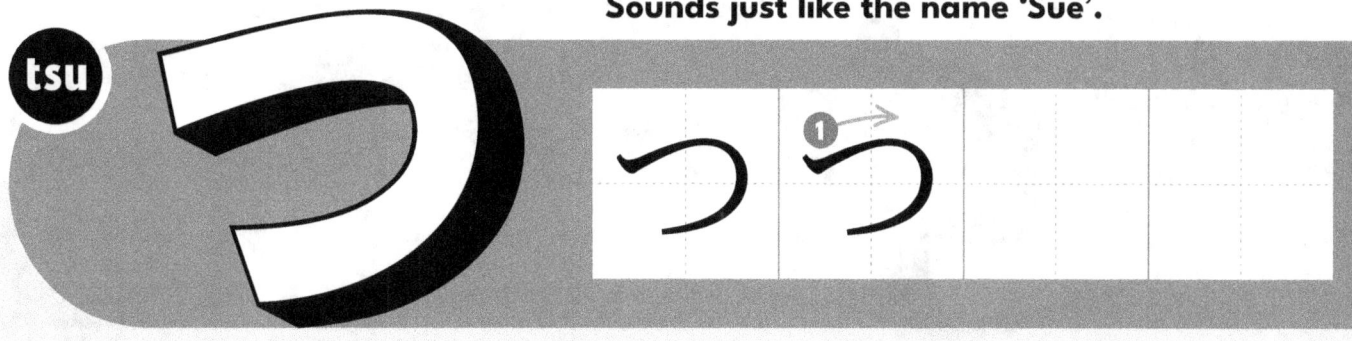

Practice writing つ by tracing these characters, with just one stroke.

Try to maintain accurate shapes while writing つ on a smaller scale.

Mnemonic.

Examples.
- A <u>tsu</u>nami wave

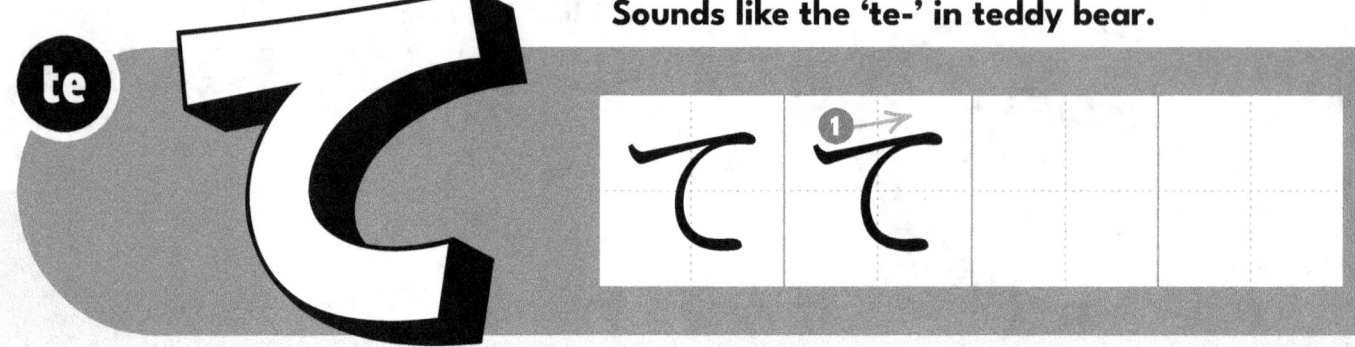

Sounds like the 'te-' in teddy bear.

Practice writing て by tracing these characters with just one stroke.

Try to maintain accurate shapes while writing て on a smaller scale.

Mnemonic.

Examples.
- Letter T for <u>t</u>en.
- <u>T</u>errible number 7

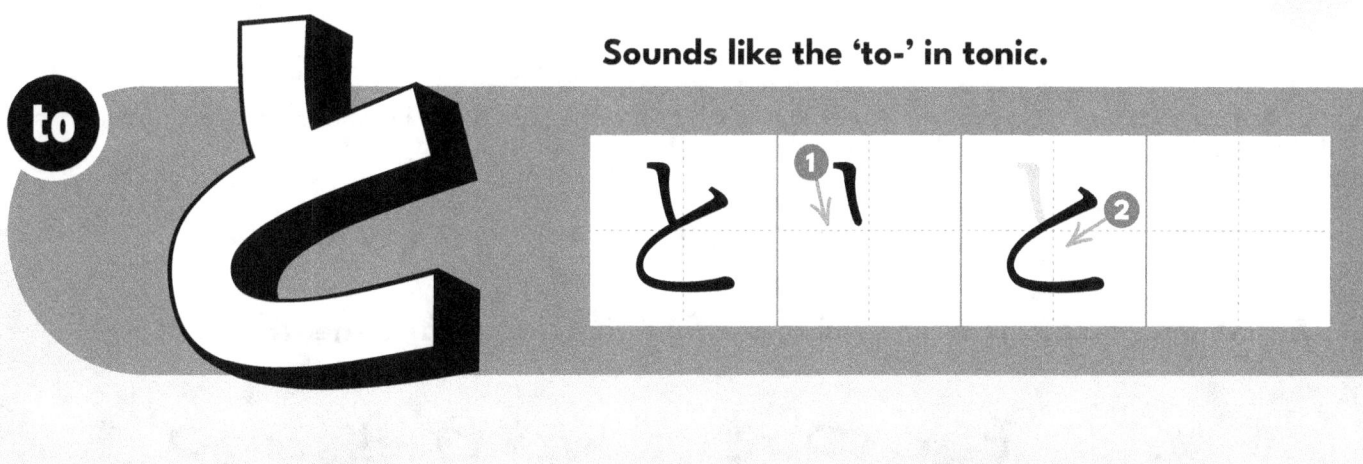

Practice writing と by tracing these characters, using **two** strokes.

Try to maintain accurate shapes while writing と on a smaller scale.

Mnemonic.

Examples.
- Picture a big <u>to</u>e with a splinter
- Imagine a thorn in your <u>to</u>ngue

These exercises will test your memorization of all twenty hiragana you have encountered. Take a break and continue.

Practice pronouncing each symbol as you write the romaji beneath.

す と く そ と つ さ う た と ち あ つ ち

そ せ え て た き け こ と ち つ こ か て

し た せ お ち さ あ す た せ い て し つ

Take a 5-minute break, and then do the same for these symbols too.

う た そ せ さ い き そ お ち か け す う

ち か て そ あ て え た け し こ と す お

せ さ う き つ え こ す と あ つ せ と し

Your brain should be saving earlier symbols to your longer-term memory, making them easier to recognize and recall.

This time, take a 10-minute break and come back to complete these.

し ち た つ あ て す か さ ち け い う え

け え さ て そ せ こ お す き と う そ し

お す き そ せ ち あ し つ と か せ た こ

After a much longer break, add the romaji for each symbol below.

お き こ す せ こ あ う け ち そ て ち す

と つ た せ け さ そ さ と お し か え し

せ ち と つ か う あ た い そ す き え た

Practice reading and writing words with characters from all group so far.

すし — sushi

つち — soil

そと — outside

さけ — sake

こと — thing

くつ — shoes

かこ — past

てつ — iron/steel

せき — cough

たつ — to stand/leave

とち — land

うた — song

かた — shoulder

しち — seven

さす — to point

あした — tomorrow

とおい — far

きせつ — season

さとい — clever

ちかてつ — subway

H5. The N & H Columns

This group is a little larger than the previous few and, largely, follows the [consonant + vowel] pattern. One symbol will immediately stand out as different. Instead of having a 'h-' sound added, like the others in this column, it is shown with 'f-' and it is pronounced with a sort of mixture of sounds - generally, this should almost sound like 'hfu-' when you pronounce it.

Symbols in this learning block.

Pronunciation

Most of this group will sound exactly how it reads. Add a regular 'n-' and 'h-' sound like those used when saying words like 'north' and 'house' to the basic vowel sounds. Both are voiced consonants, and the 'n-' sounds are nasal sounding.

The pronunciation of ふ is a little odd and may be sound like 'fu' and 'hu' depending on use. Generally, this has a 'hfu' sound that is made by trying to say 'foo' without your teeth making contact with your lip. You still need to bring your lips closer together but the huff of air is expelled through open lips, instead of the puff of air generated by touching your lip against the upper teeth.

Sounds just like the '-na's in banana

Practice writing な **by tracing these characters, using** **four** **strokes.**

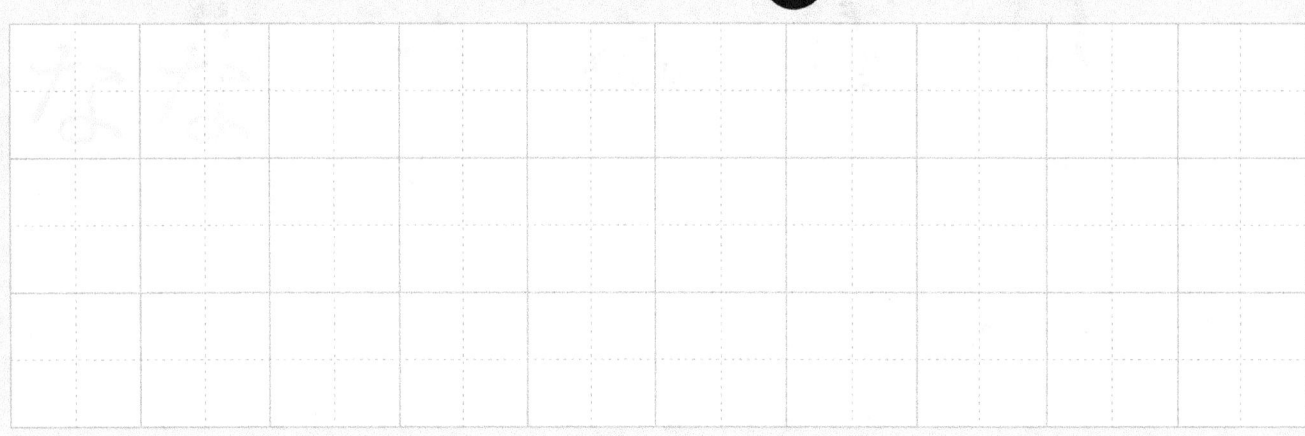

Try to maintain accurate shapes while writing な **on a smaller scale.**

Mnemonic.

Examples.
- A <u>na</u>ughty person, praying at a cross.

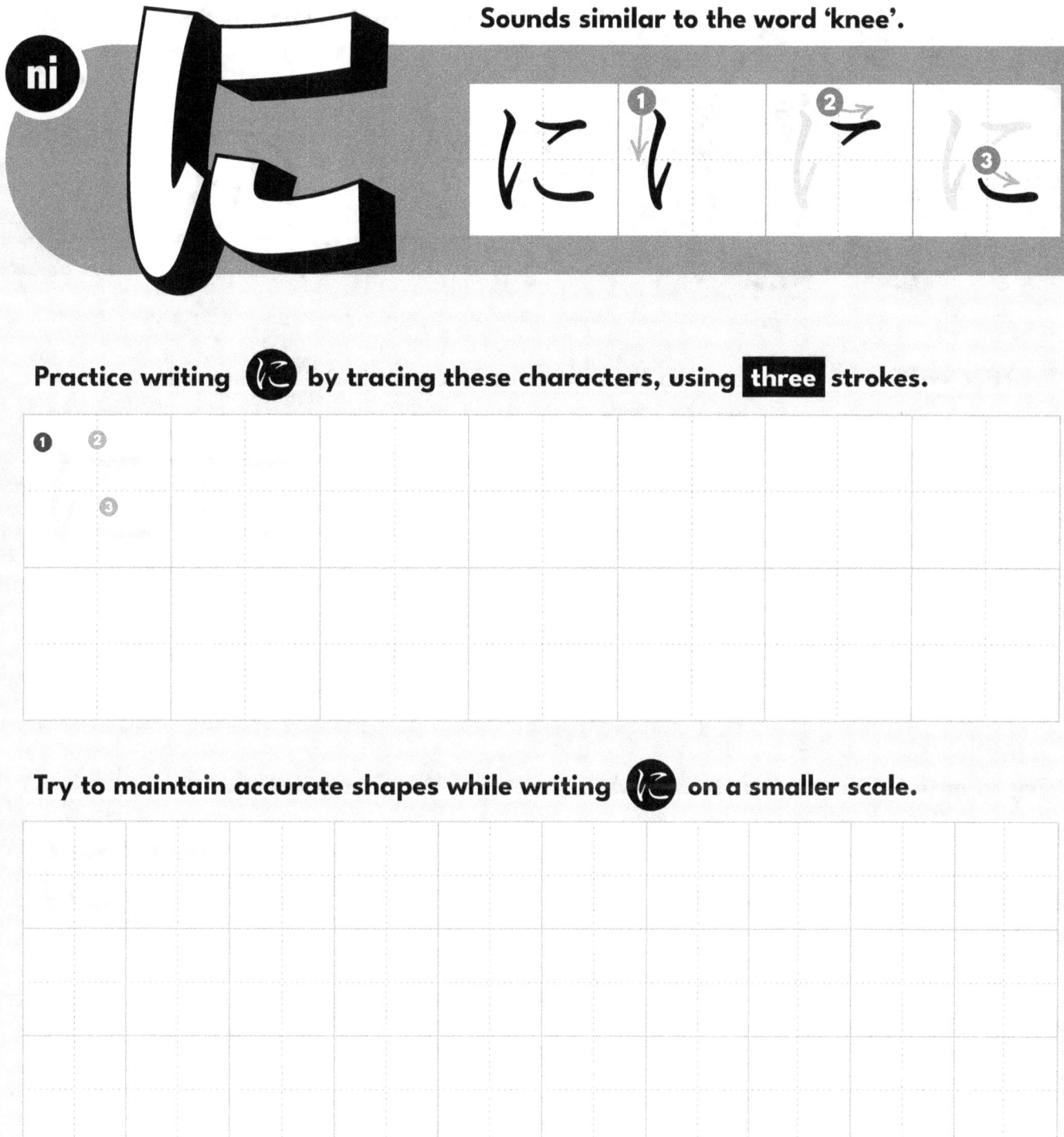

Practice writing に **by tracing these characters, using three strokes.**

Try to maintain accurate shapes while writing に **on a smaller scale.**

Mnemonic.

Examples.
- Picture as a <u>knee</u>
- <u>Nearly</u> a square?

nu — ぬ

Sounds like the 'noo' in the word noon.

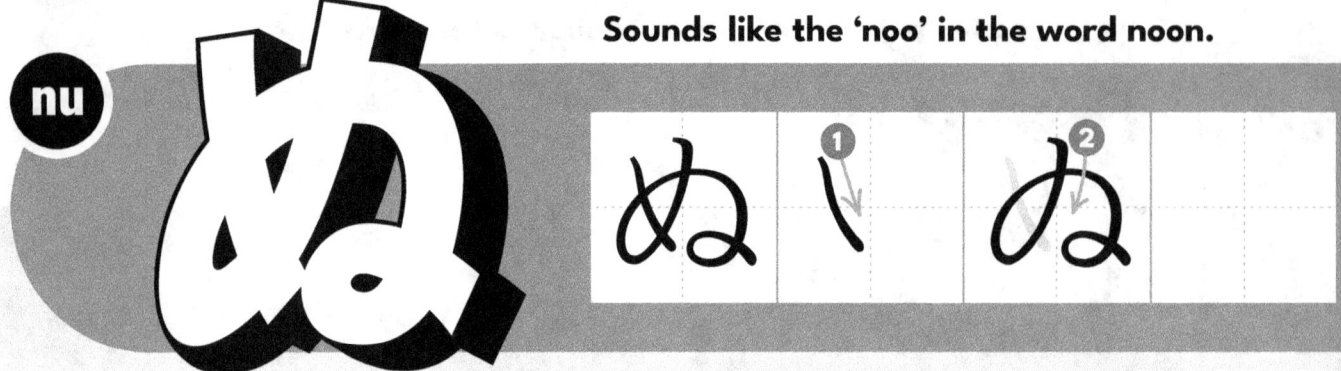

Practice writing ぬ by tracing these characters with just two strokes.

Try to maintain accurate shapes while writing ぬ on a smaller scale.

Mnemonic.

Examples.
- A bowl of <u>noo</u>dles with chopsticks
- A clockface, and it's almost <u>noon</u>

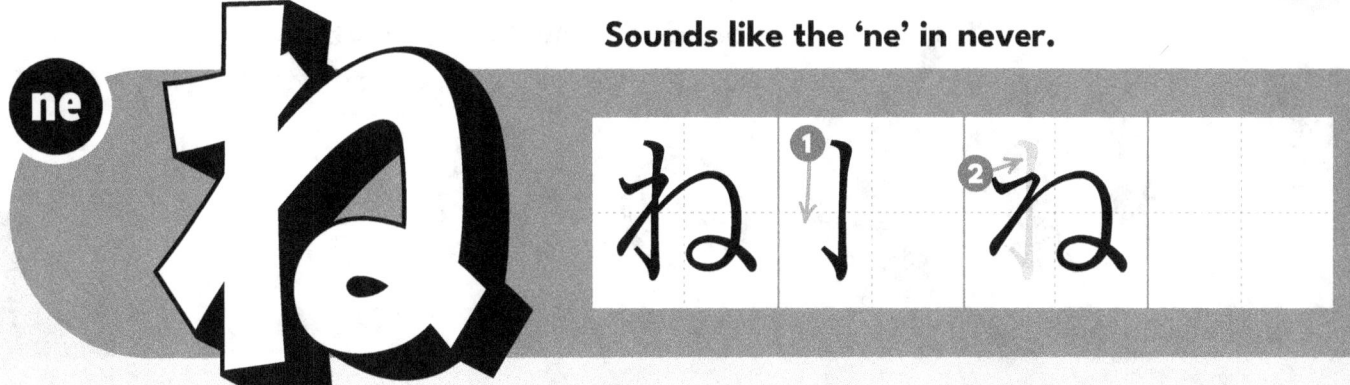

Sounds like the 'ne' in never.

Practice writing ね by tracing these characters, using two strokes.

Try to maintain accurate shapes while writing ね on a smaller scale.

Mnemonic.

Examples.
- <u>Ne</u>lly the elephant, with a curly trunk
- A cat, curled up, or '<u>ne</u>ko' in Japanese

no

Sounds like the 'no-' in north.

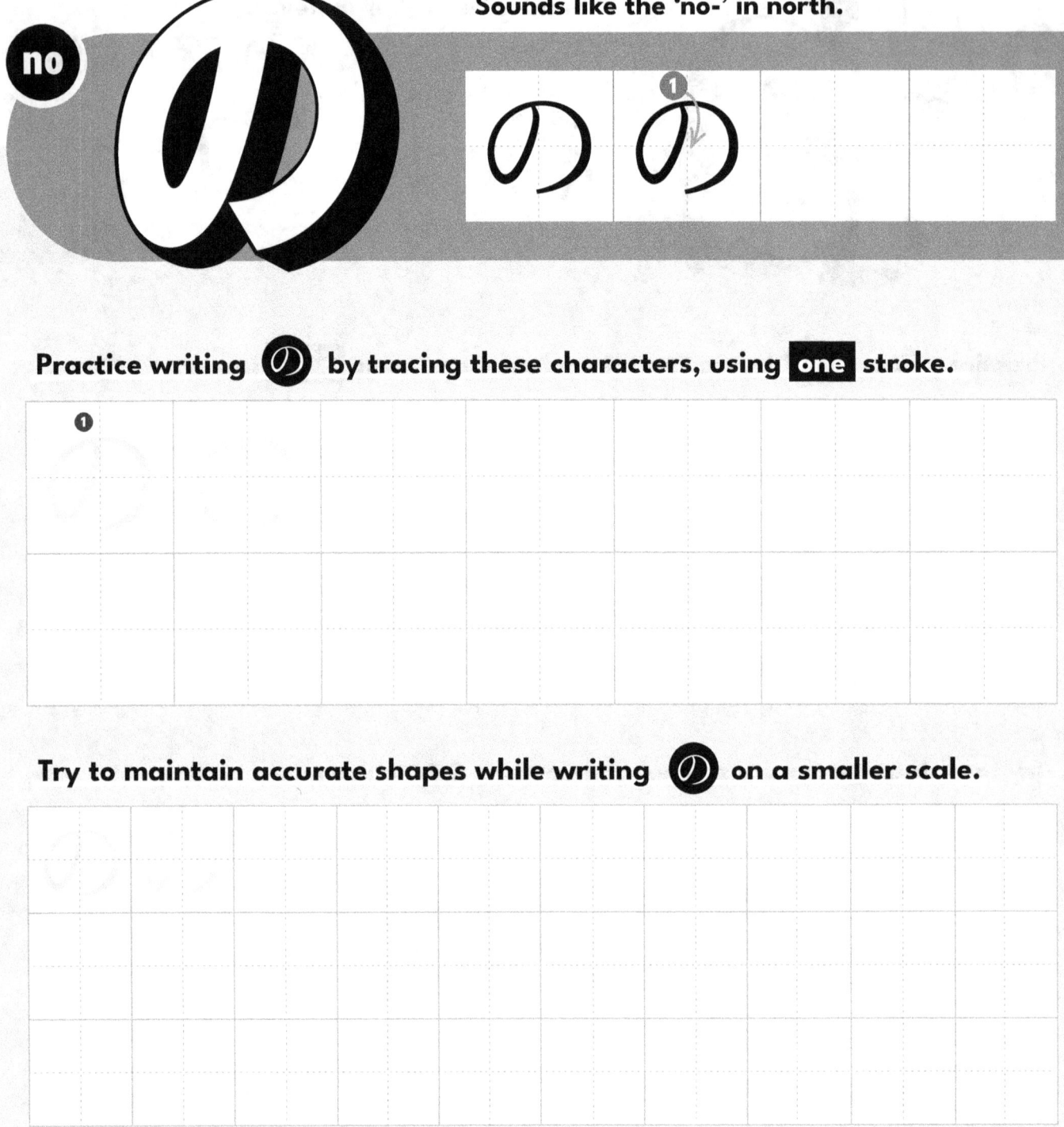

Practice writing の **by tracing these characters, using** **one** **stroke.**

Try to maintain accurate shapes while writing の **on a smaller scale.**

Mnemonic.

Examples.

- A pigs <u>no</u>se
- A sign that says <u>NO</u> Smoking

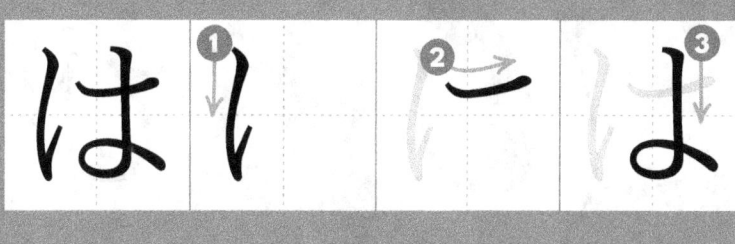

Pronounce as 'ha' like in hand.

Practice writing は by tracing these characters, using **three** strokes.

Try to maintain accurate shapes while writing は on a smaller scale.

Mnemonic.

Examples.
- Looks like letters 'h' and 'a', for '<u>ha</u>'

Practice writing ひ by tracing these characters with just one stroke.

Try to maintain accurate shapes while writing ひ on a smaller scale.

Mnemonic.

Examples.
- Big smile, laughing mouth, "hee hee!"
- Like a mans nose, He has a big nose

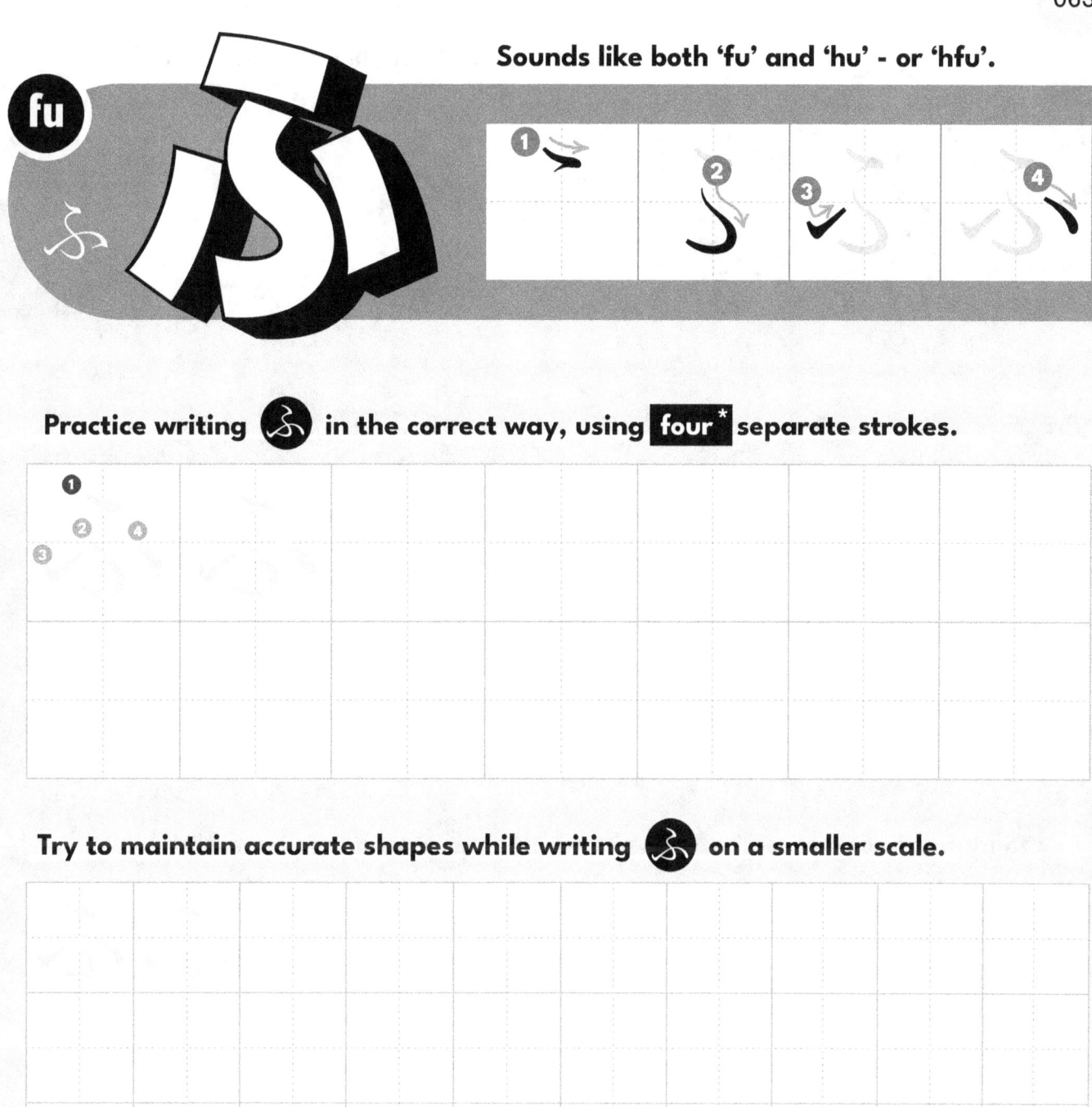

Sounds like both 'fu' and 'hu' - or 'hfu'.

fu

Practice writing ふ in the correct way, using **four*** separate strokes.

Try to maintain accurate shapes while writing ふ on a smaller scale.

Mnemonic.

Examples.
- Imagine Mount <u>Fu</u>ji
- Can you picture a <u>hu</u>la dancer?
- Upside-down, <u>who</u>?

he

Pronounce as 'heh', like the 'he-' in hello!

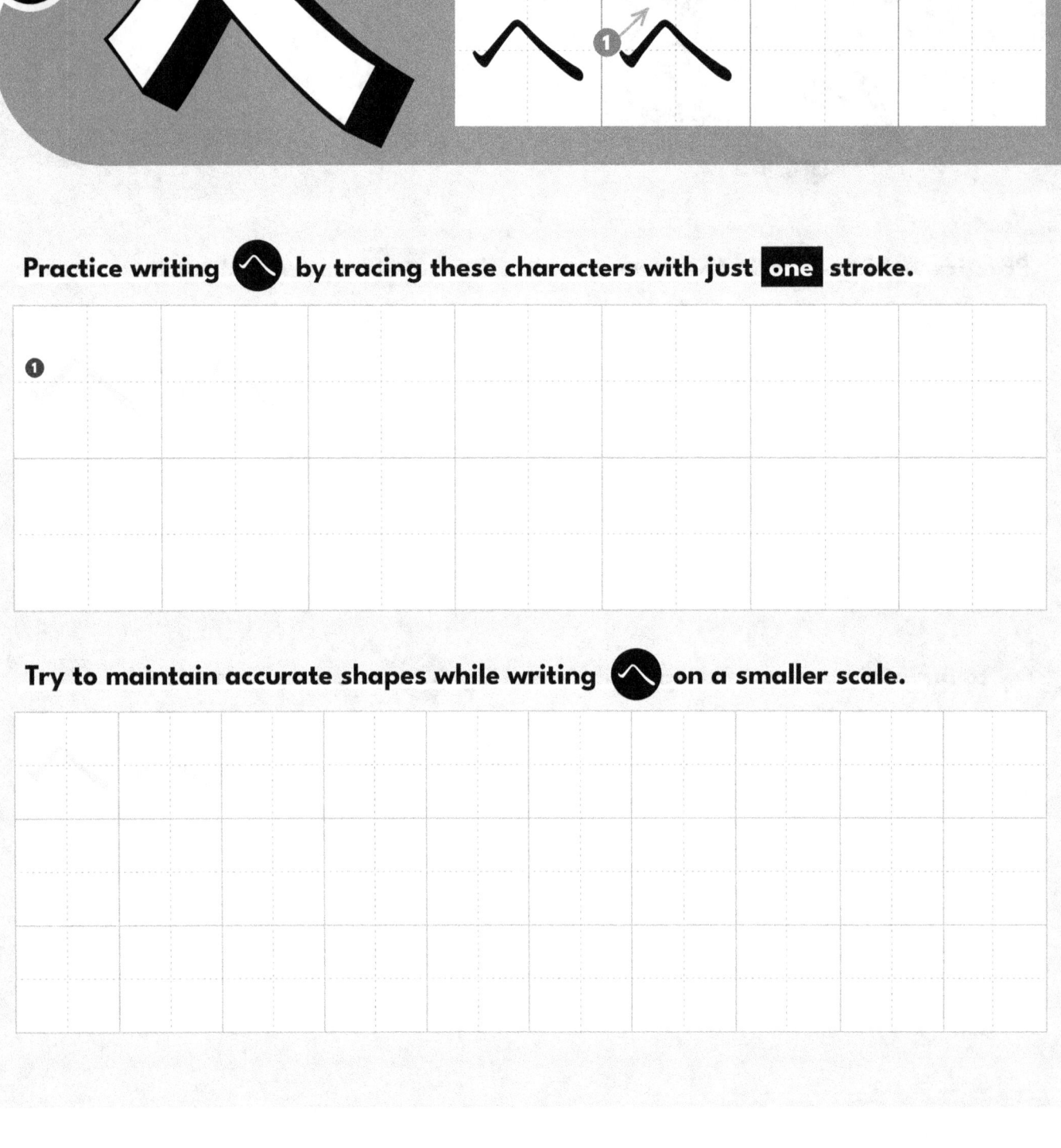

Practice writing ヘ by tracing these characters with just one stroke.

Try to maintain accurate shapes while writing ヘ on a smaller scale.

Mnemonic.

Examples.
- Points to <u>he</u>aven
- <u>He</u>y, that's easy to write

Pronounce like the 'ho-' in horse.

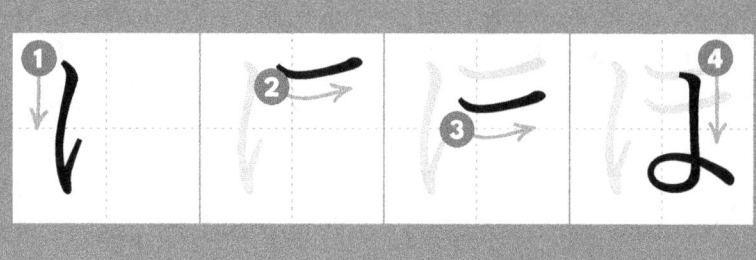

Practice writing ほ by tracing these characters, using four strokes.

Try to maintain accurate shapes while writing ほ on a smaller scale.

Mnemonic.

Examples.

- 'ha' with a hat =
  Santa! Ho ho <u>ho</u>!
- A w<u>ho</u>le lot of lines.

Even after learning a large group of new characters, this may start to feel easier each time. That's a good thing!

Practice pronouncing each symbol as you write the romaji beneath.

に な ほ は ち そ へ は そ す ひ の と せ

へ く つ ひ ね あ て こ な ふ し ほ へ は

ぬ ふ の す ち ふ ほ つ き お ひ に た さ

Take a 5-minute break, and then do the same for these symbols too.

せ つ う へ き え さ こ あ し す そ の い

な か け ひ ね た は す ぬ く け せ ふ ほ

に と お い の ほ そ く し あ え こ き て

You could make this more challenging by introducing a time limit for each group and reducing it for each set. Try to improve from one group to the next.

This time, take a 10-minute break and come back to complete these.

この な あ ぬ く つ た え う に ほ ぬ ね

せ と ち ひ へ き ふ そ す に ね け ひ は

か の お へ ほ ふ へ ぬ さ は て い な ほ

After a much longer break, add the romaji for each symbol below.

ふ の ぬ あ て ほ な へ そ へ た こ は ね

つ き に ひ せ と い ひ へ な ぬ な さ は

す ほ ち し ぬ け う に お さ ほ か の ふ

Practice reading and writing words with all the characters so far.

なに — what

ほね — bone

ぬの — cloth

ひふ — skin

へた — unskillful

はな — nose/flower

ふね — ship

かに — crab

ひな — doll/fledgling

はし — chopsticks/bridge

きぬ — silk

ほし — star

ひと — person

のき — eaves

にし — west

はいく — Haiku

かたな — Katana

せいふ — government

いのしし — boar

へいそつ — soldier

H6. The M & Y Columns

Two more columns coming up in this section. The two symbols that seem to be 'missing' from the Y column *(YE and YI)* sounded similar enough to the vowel-only column that the Japanese dropped them altogether (い & え). This just simplified the alphabet, meaning fewer symbols to learn!

Symbols in this learning block.

Pronunciation

The *'m-'* sounds are pronounced in virtually the same way as in English, bringing your lips together, voiced *(your vocal chords are used)*, and nasal like *'n-'* sounds.

The *'y-'* sound characters are very much like the English pronunciation and you will notice that there are only three to learn. It is possible to hear the occasional *'ye'* but this is usually limited to foreign words and so isn't a sound that you need to learn for the Japanese language.

Sounds like 'ma-' in the word man.

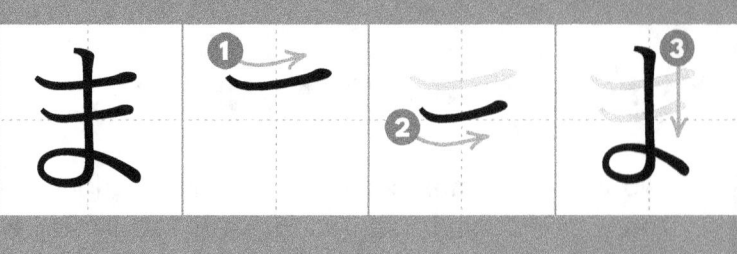

Practice writing ま by tracing these characters, using three strokes.

Try to maintain accurate shapes while writing ま on a smaller scale.

Mnemonic.

Examples.
- Magma, exploding from a volcano
- Looks mathematical

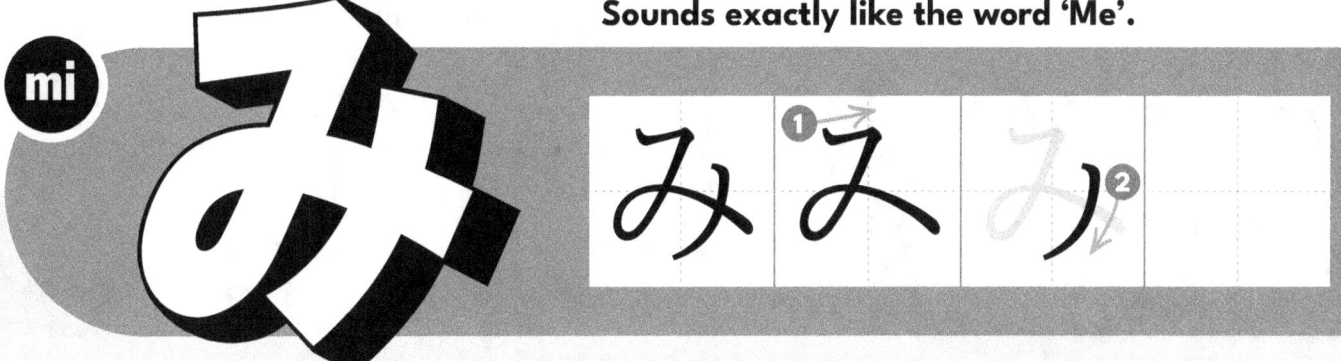

mi — Sounds exactly like the word 'Me'.

Practice writing み by tracing these characters, using **two** strokes.

Try to maintain accurate shapes while writing み on a smaller scale.

Mnemonic.

Examples.
- Looks like 21 to <u>me</u>.
- Who wishes to be aged 21 again? <u>Me</u>!

mu — む

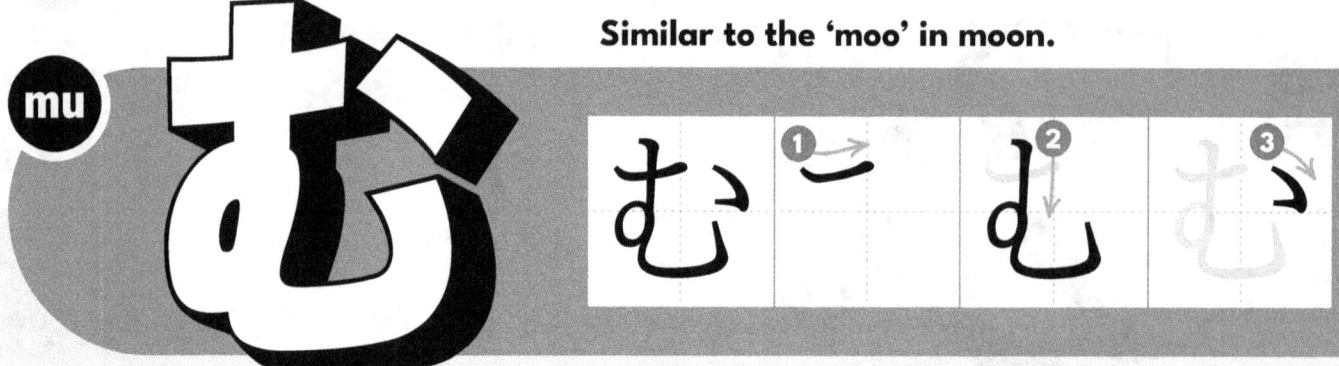

Similar to the 'moo' in moon.

Practice writing む **by tracing these characters, using three strokes.**

Try to maintain accurate shapes while writing む **on a smaller scale.**

Mnemonic.

Examples.
- Picture the shape of a cow... <u>Moo</u>!
- A projector, showing a <u>movie</u>?

Sounds like the 'me-' in men.

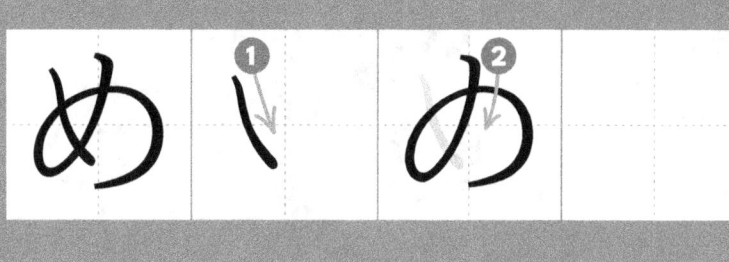

Practice writing め by tracing these characters, using **two** strokes.

Try to maintain accurate shapes while writing め on a smaller scale.

Mnemonic.

Examples.

- Like an eye, which is '<u>me</u>' in Japanese
- Like 'nu' for noodles, but not as <u>me</u>ssy.

Sounds similar to the 'mo-' in monsoon.

Practice writing も by tracing these characters, using three strokes.

Try to maintain accurate shapes while writing も on a smaller scale.

Mnemonic.

Examples.
- A fishing hook with <u>mo</u>re worms.
- You will catch <u>mo</u>re fish with this hook.

Sounds much like the 'ya-' in yak.

Practice writing や by tracing these characters, using three strokes.

Try to maintain accurate shapes while writing や on a smaller scale.

Mnemonic.

Examples.
- Picture the shape of a <u>ya</u>k's head
- Maybe the sail from a <u>ya</u>cht?

Sounds just like the word 'You'.

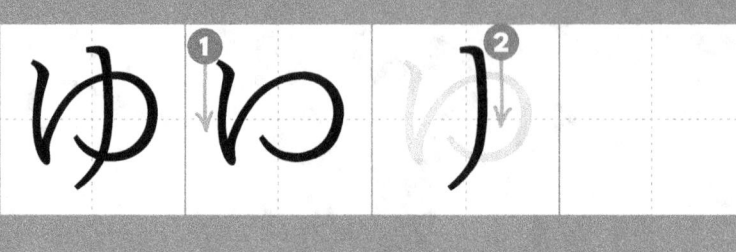

Practice writing ゆ by tracing these characters, using two strokes.

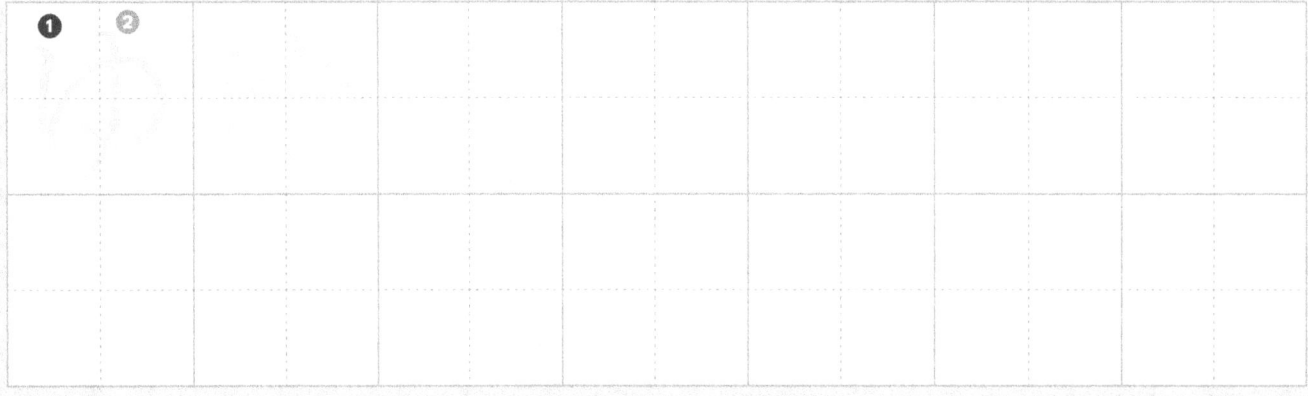

Try to maintain accurate shapes while writing ゆ on a smaller scale.

Mnemonic.

Examples.

- Combines letters that spell '<u>you</u>'
- Pict<u>u</u>re a new and <u>u</u>nique fish

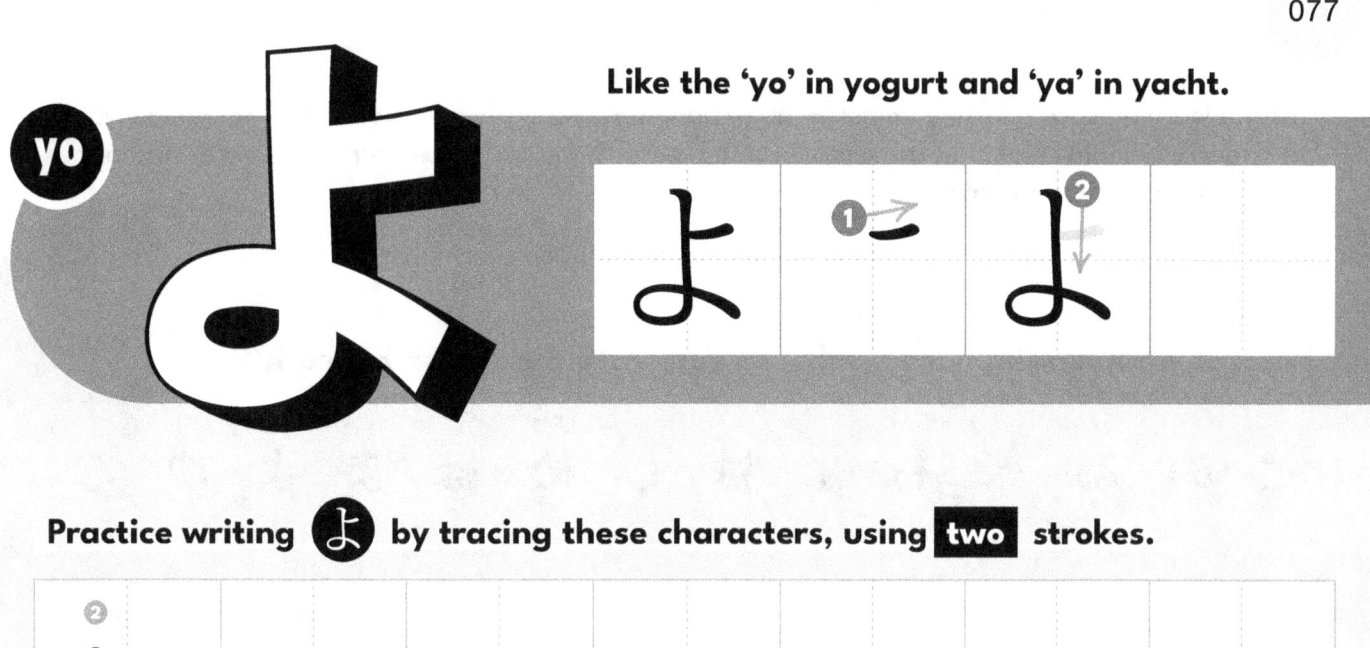

Like the 'yo' in yogurt and 'ya' in yacht.

Practice writing よ by tracing these characters, using **two** strokes.

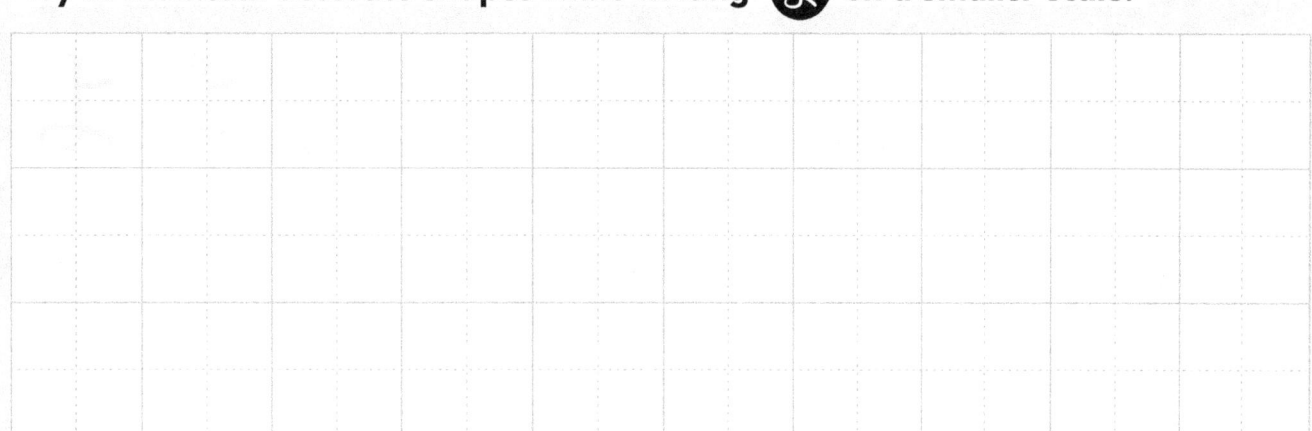

Try to maintain accurate shapes while writing よ on a smaller scale.

Mnemonic.

Examples.

- A new <u>yo</u>-yo trick?
- A hitch-hiker needs a ride, he yells "<u>yo!</u>"

Despite learning such a large number of new characters, repetition of characters that you learned much earlier should mean they are firmly in your memory. You can focus your efforts on ensuring the newer ones are sinking in too.

Practice pronouncing each symbol as you write the romaji beneath.

と め あ へ も よ は し め ほ ま よ ゆ な

ひ の む ま え ぬ む ふ ま よ ち や ほ は

ぬ や ね ゆ み に も や ふ み ね な み に

Take a 5-minute break, and then do the same for these symbols too.

め む き ほ や と よ せ つ そ に も ゆ ほ

た み て ね の ま は お ひ す な く ね も

や ぬ よ む め な ゆ は ぬ う へ に み ふ

This time, take a 10-minute break and come back to complete these.

し ね か や と い ぬ す へ つ ゆ た そ さ

ま ひ く せ え な て め に こ せ こ の よ

み あ も か し ち き お う く ふ む お い

After a much longer break, add the romaji for each symbol below.

け め て ち え ゆ け す お き い か や さ

ひ ぬ む も へ ふ せ の く こ せ た み と

し は う ほ つ そ ま そ な よ お に ね い

The words below are all written with syllables you have now studied.

やま — mountain
ゆめ — to dream
よむ — to read
もも — peach
みや — shrine
こめ — uncooked rice
つゆ — dew
むし — insect
まつ — to wait/pine tree
うめ — plum

むね — chest, breast
きもの — kimono
さしみ — sashimi
ゆかた — cotton kimono
えまき — picture scroll
みこし — portable shrine
うきよえ — woodblock print
せともの — porcelain
すきやき — sukiyaki

H7. The R Column

The romaji letter *'r'* is a poor substitute for the Japanese *'r-'* sound and pronunciation of characters in this column can be difficult to master. It is a mixture of romaji letter sounds that is only two thirds *'r'*. A quarter of the sound feels like a lower case *'l' (as in 'learn')*, and the remainder almost a lower case *'d'* sound *(like in 'dark')*.

Symbols in this learning block.

Pronunciation

Combining the sounds of three letters in one is tricky. We found the exercise below can help English speakers to understand and produce an accurate Japanese *'r-'* sound:

Begin with a regular *'l'* sound, saying *'La'* out loud a few times. Your tongue will point upwards a little so that the bottom of it makes contact with the roof of your mouth. Say *'La'* a few more times, paying attention to the position of your tongue and location that it makes contacts with the top of your mouth. *"La. La. La"*.

Now do the same with a *'d'* sound, saying *'Da'* until you can feel exactly where your tongue is touching the inside of your mouth. Your tongue will have a much flatter shape and forward position, touching the back of your upper front teeth. *"Da. Da. Da"*.

Finally, alternate between saying *'La'* and *'Da'*, paying attention to the placement of your tongue. Both positions should be the same as in the steps above. As your tongue moves back and forth, you may begin to notice that your it skips over the same spot each time. *"La. Da. La. Da"*.

The Japanese *'r'* sound is made by positioning the tongue in that space between *'La'* and *'Da'*. It takes some getting used to but with enough practice, muscle memory will take over. Simply follow these same steps for the other vowel sounds, swapping out the 'a' sound each time. *"Li, Di"... "Lu, Du"... and so on.*

ra — Sounds a lot like the 'ra-' in rabbit.

Practice writing ら by tracing these characters, using two strokes.

Try to maintain accurate shapes while writing ら on a smaller scale.

Mnemonic.

Examples.
- Imagine the shape of a <u>rabbit</u>
- Maybe the number 5 but it's a bit <u>rattled</u>

Sounds a lot like the 'rea-' in reach.

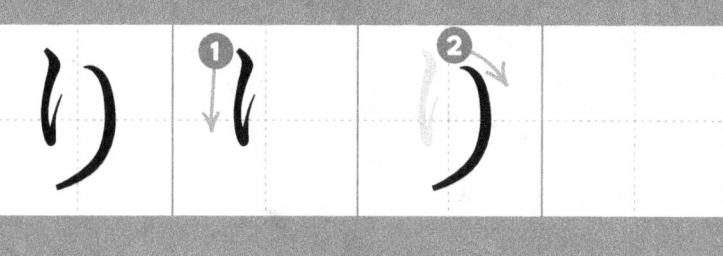

Practice writing り by tracing these characters, using two strokes.

Try to maintain accurate shapes while writing り on a smaller scale.

Mnemonic.

Examples.
- Two <u>rea</u>ching arms
- Maybe two <u>ree</u>ds

Sounds like the '-ru' in guru.

Practice writing る **by tracing these characters with just** one **stroke.**

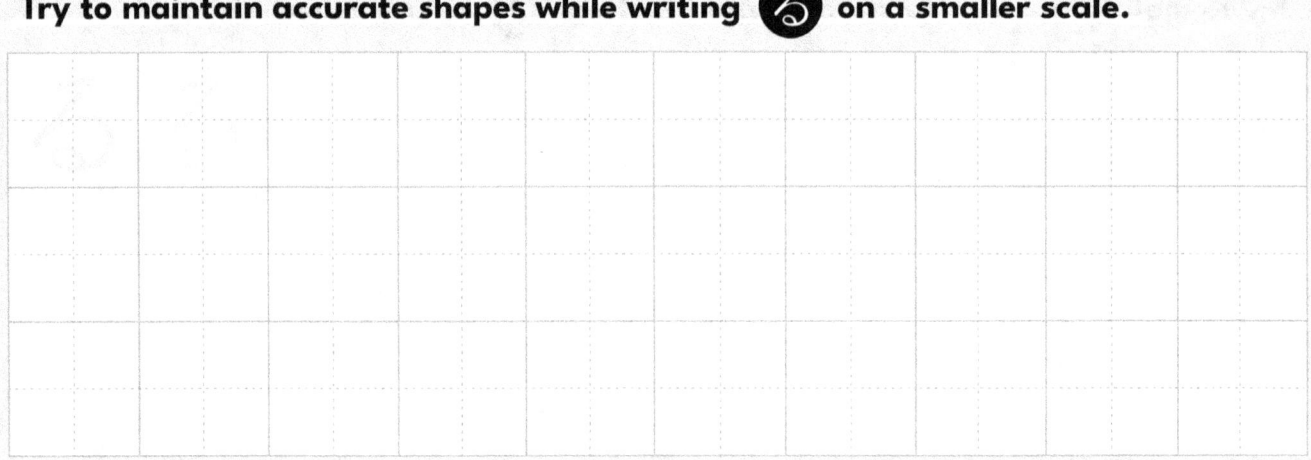

Try to maintain accurate shapes while writing る **on a smaller scale.**

Mnemonic.

Examples.
- Rope, with a loop
- As roads go, this is the scenic route.

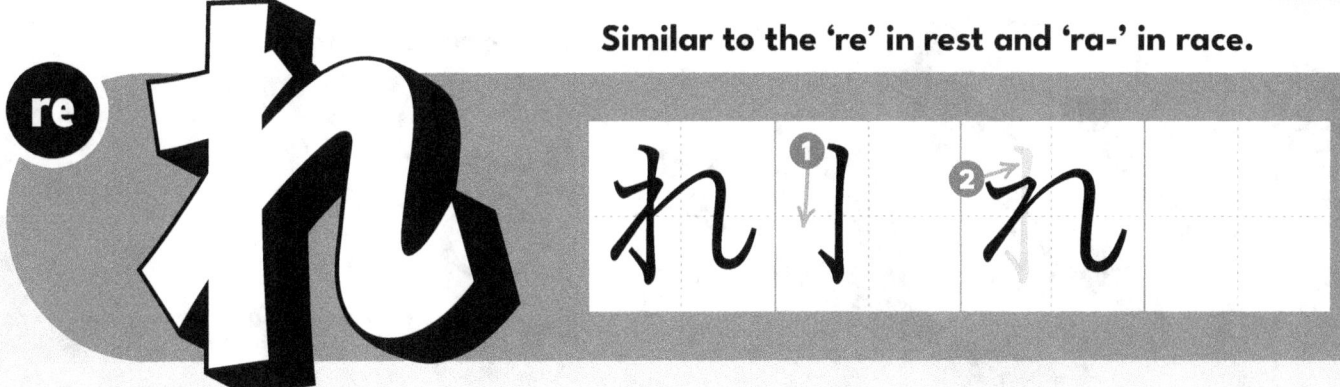

Similar to the 're' in rest and 'ra-' in race.

Practice writing れ by tracing these characters, using **two** strokes.

Try to maintain accurate shapes while writing れ on a smaller scale.

Mnemonic.

Examples.
- A <u>re</u>ace across the finish line
- Picture a snake, <u>re</u>sting on a branch

ro ろ

Sounds like the '-rro' in churro.

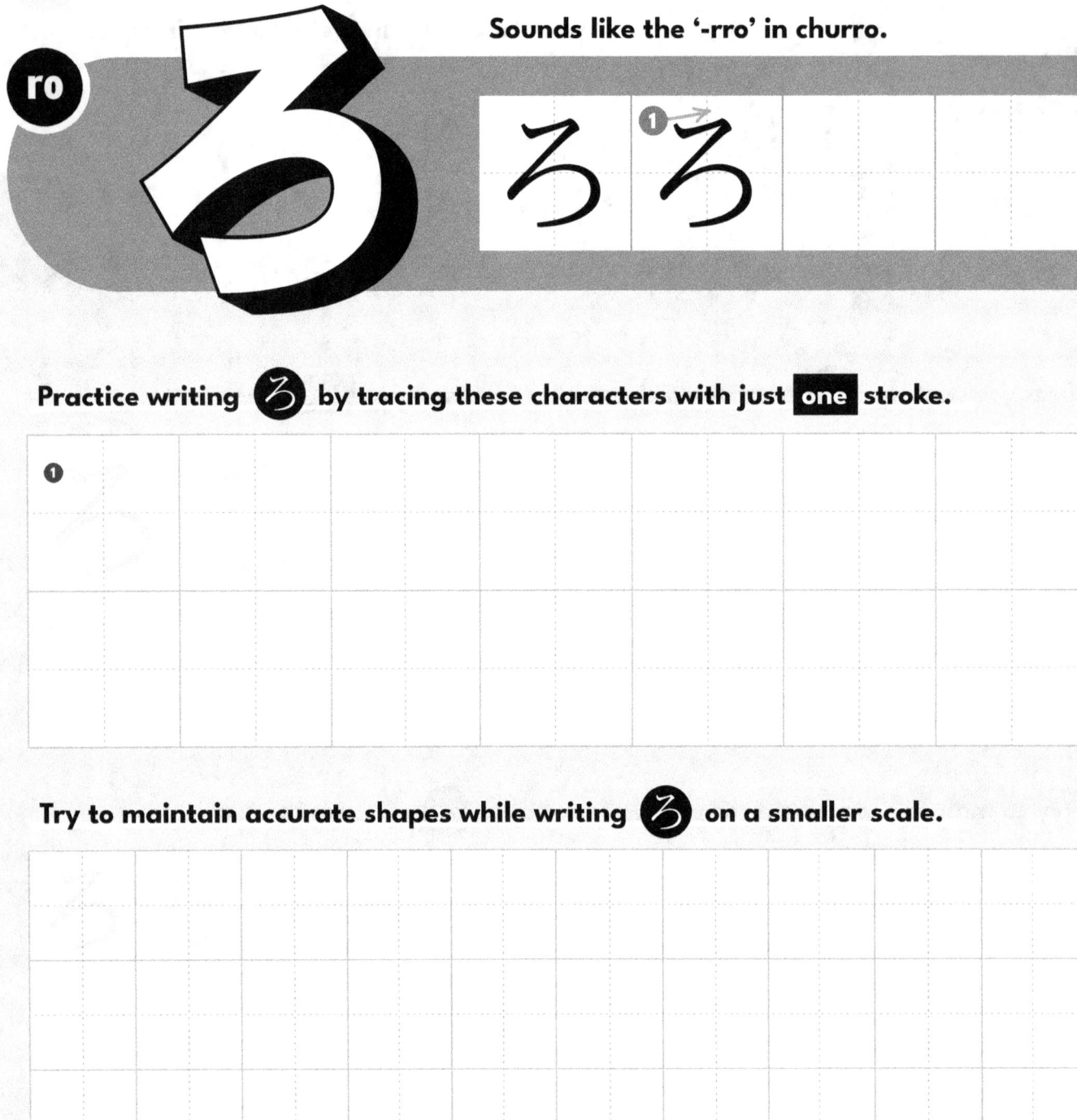

Practice writing ろ by tracing these characters with just one stroke.

Try to maintain accurate shapes while writing ろ on a smaller scale.

Mnemonic.

Examples.
- This <u>ro</u>ad is less bendy than in 'ru'
- <u>Ro</u>pe, but no loop

H8. The W Column + N

This last block of hiragana has just three characters to learn. The first is relatively normal but the second and third are a little different. The *'w-'* is quite close to the *'u'*, and should be pronounced this way. The last symbol doesn't actually have any vowel sound but needed to be placed in a group:

Symbols in this learning block:

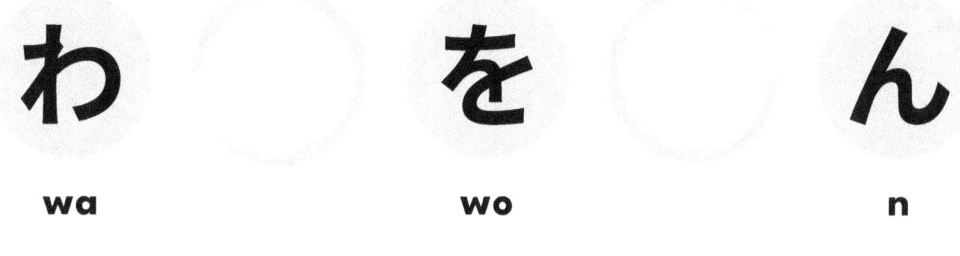

wa   wo   n

Pronunciation

As mentioned above, the *'w-'* characters are pronounced in a similar way to the vowel sounds for 'u' and less like the letter *'w'* in English. Your lips should not be pushed out as they would if saying *'oo'* but they do need to be compressed. When pronouncing *'wa'*, it should almost sound like *'oo-wah'* and taking the same length of time to say as any other symbol.

The sound of *'wo'* is similar, sounding like *'oo-woh'*. This character is mainly found in use as a particle.

Unlike all the other kana you have learned, the Japanese *'n'* character ん has no vowel sound attached to it. Pronounce this as *'nnn'*, as it sounds in ten or rain.

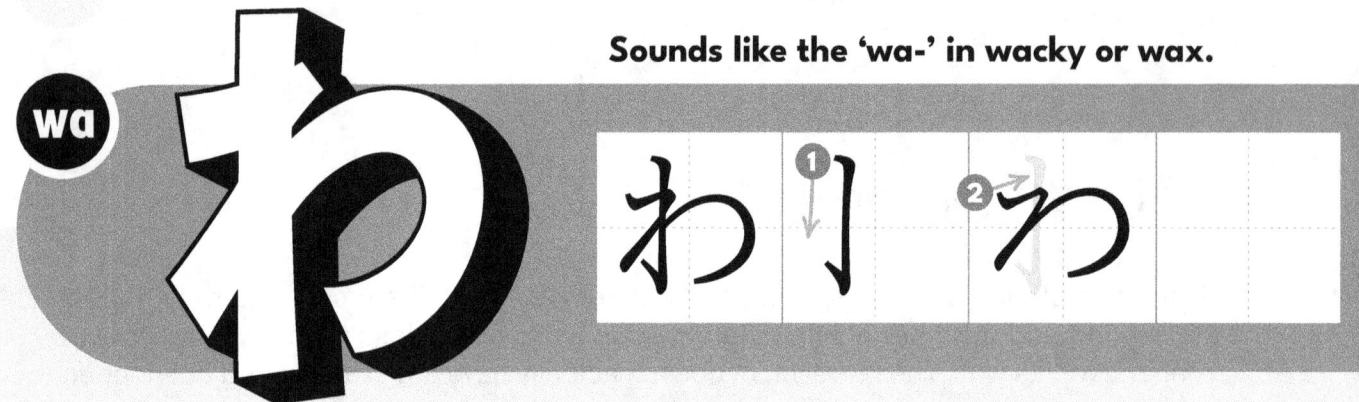

Sounds like the 'wa-' in wacky or wax.

Practice writing わ **by tracing these characters, using two strokes.**

Try to maintain accurate shapes while writing わ **on a smaller scale.**

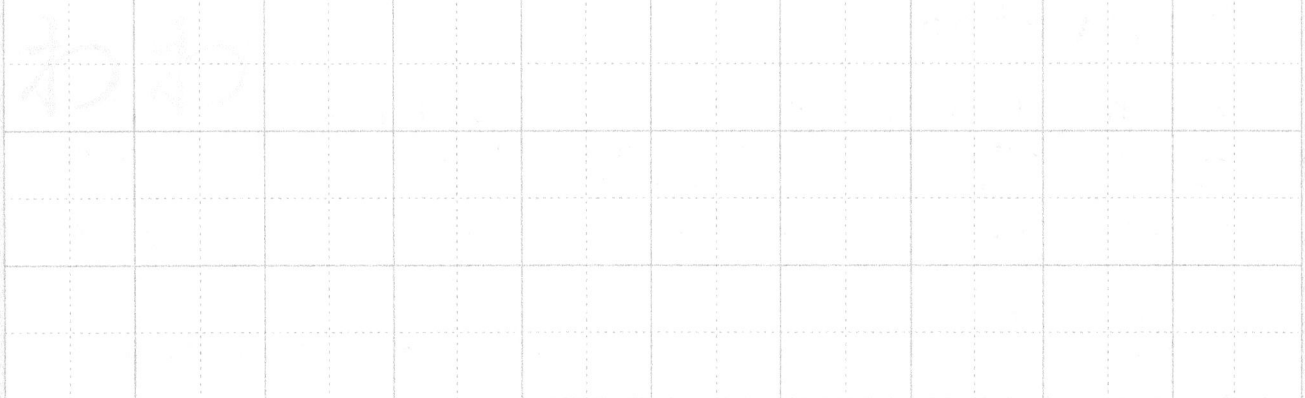

Mnemonic.

Examples.

- Picture a <u>wa</u>sp, crawling up a tree
- Maybe a <u>wa</u>iter, and their big, round tray

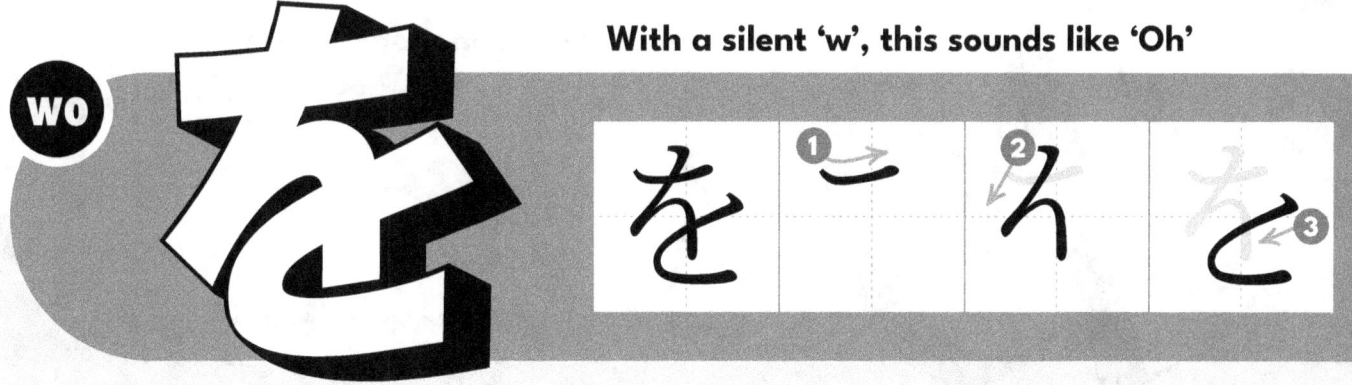

WO — With a silent 'w', this sounds like 'Oh'

Practice writing を by tracing these characters, using three strokes.

Try to maintain accurate shapes while writing を on a smaller scale.

Mnemonic.

Examples.
- Dipping a toe in a cold pond… "woah"
- Picture a cowboy on a horse… "woah"

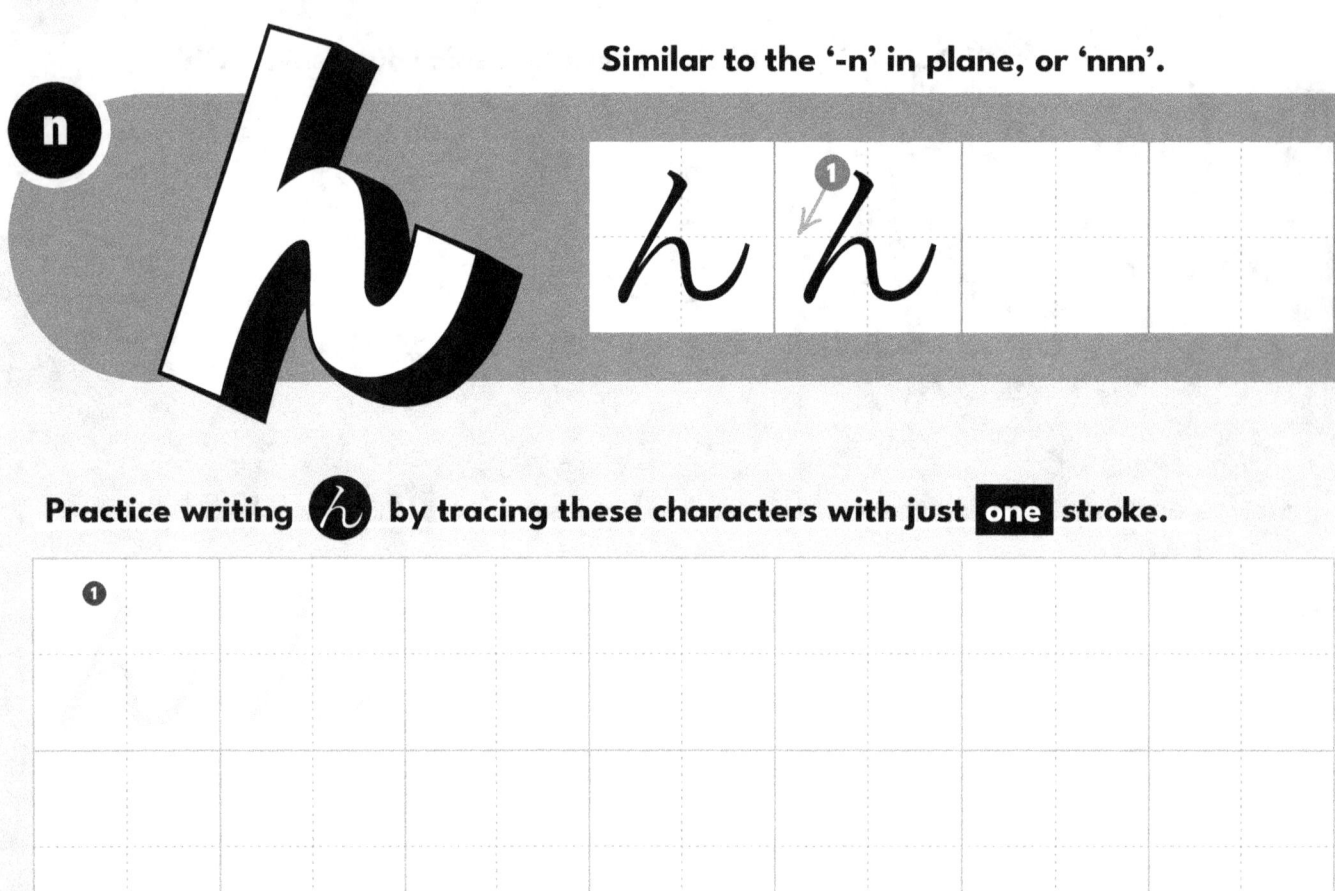

n

Similar to the '-n' in plane, or 'nnn'.

Practice writing ん by tracing these characters with just one stroke.

Try to maintain accurate shapes while writing ん on a smaller scale.

Mnemonic.

Examples.
- Lower case letter 'n'
- The last hiragana, at the end.

That last group completes the set, meaning this exercise may contain any of the 46 hiragana. Most should be familiar by now; write the romaji below characters from all groups below.

Practice pronouncing each symbol as you write the romaji beneath.

り　む　を　ろ　ほ　み　ん　さ　ま　ゆ　ち　ら　ろ　よ

わ　ろ　も　よ　れ　む　ん　と　ん　り　る　く　み　る

れ　る　ら　り　も　や　ま　め　を　け　れ　わ　め　や

Take a 5-minute break, and then do the same for these symbols too.

て　ゆ　ら　ほ　へ　む　け　は　す　う　ろ　く　ね　や

る　い　の　き　お　か　あ　を　に　ち　も　し　つ　こ

そ　ひ　ら　わ　を　ふ　れ　み　な　り　ま　え　さ　め

This time, take a 10-minute break and come back to complete these.

ひ ら ん そ り ぬ た む わ る れ ろ に ら

み め ゆ る や へ え も よ す く む ま ん

ろ を め も ま ほ つ の み は ふ あ れ わ

After a much longer break, add the romaji for each symbol below.

ゆ よ や を ね た ん せ と ゆ ら わ あ を

ほ よ に む も る り み つ ら れ ろ を す

は を ひ ん や ね わ の る ゆ く め も ふ

These final word lists may contain characters from all hiragana study blocks.

わん
bay/bowl

てら
temple

つる
crane / to fish

これ
this

ふろ
bath

のり
seaweed/glue

はる
to stretch

れい
example/soul

しろ
castle/white

にほん
Japan

さくら
cherry blossom

うちわ
round fan

まつり
festival

ほたる
firefly

ふとん
futon

れきし
history

わふく
Japanese clothing

りろん
theory

ひのまる
Rising Sun flag

さむらい
Samurai

///////////////////////////////// **PART 3**

Additional Sounds

The basic kana characters cover a lot of the syllable sounds that we need to pronounce Japanese, but not all of them. Both sets of letters that you have just learned can be adapted with some extra annotation, to show when the sound that is normally used will need to be altered. When one of these different sounds is required the existing sets of letters are accompanied by either small marks or even extra kana. The next few pages will show you what these differences are, and how the sounds can be adapted.

Voiced Consonants

An additional set of *'voiced'* sounds are created by altering how we pronounce certain consonant sounds. The modified sounds are similar to their original, except that they require vibration in your vocal cords. Essentially, one of the basic consonant sounds is replaced by another, illustrated with a different *Romaji* letter.

Basic consonant sounds, such as *t-*, *s-*, and *k-*, are produced without your voice box, as the movement of air creates these sounds. You can check this by making a *'t-'* sound once or twice - *remember, it's not the letter 'T' or "tee,"* but a short *'t-'* sound. These are 'voiceless' consonants, and we refer to kana such as か *(ka)* and た *(ta)* in the same way. The modified, 'voiced' versions are made with the same mouth shapes but also by adding *your voice*. For example, the *'k-'* in か *(ka)* becomes a *'g-,'* and *'t-'* changes into *'d-.'*

In written Japanese, existing kana characters with different pronunciations have extra **diacritic marks**. In this case, they are also referred to as *'voicing marks'* as the new, modified consonant sounds are *'voiced'* versions of their initial form. **Dakuten** are two extra lines that we draw in the upper right, similar to quotation marks, and a small circle in the same position is called **handakuten**.

Dakuten are attached to symbols that begin with *k*, *t*, s, and *h- sounds,* while only those starting with *h-* sounds have *handakuten*. Diacritic marks are written after all other strokes have been drawn.

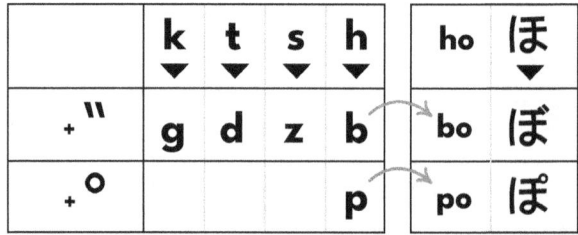

Voicing marks have been added to the basic hiragana - displayed to the right.

Romaji does not accurately illustrate Japanese sounds, so some characters are marked with an asterisk* to show variation from overall patterns. A 'French' 'j-' sound is better suited to 'chi' and 'shi,' while 'z-' or 'dz-' sounds are closer matches for 'tsu' and 'su.'

Hiragana

Combination Hiragana

Also referred to as **compound kana**, these are the written representations of hybrid sounds made by combining two others. Essentially, an extra consonant sound is added to the front of another character. The most important thing to remember is that while we write them with two kana, they take **one mora** to say.

The rules for writing *compound kana* are the same for both hiragana and katakana scripts, including the new characters for *'voiced'* sounds from the previous pages.

The written form consists of one regular-sized character that usually ends with an *'-i'* sound, such as し *(shi)*, き *(ki)*, ち *(chi)*, etc., and a second, small character, typically や *(ya)*, ゆ *(yu)*, or よ *(yo)*:

き + よ = きょ
ki　yo　kyo

Compound kana are used in writing completely different words to their equivalent, normal-sized counterparts. The difference in character size is more apparent when comparing words that are written using the same characters:

きよう
ki-yo-u　'skillful'

きょう
kyo-u　'today'

A single mora can change the meaning of a word, but they are relatively easy to recognize with practice. A mispronounced or misheard compound sound can have a significant impact on the meaning of what is said:

The chart on the next page shows the most common hybrid sounds, combining an initial character ending in an *'-i'* sound with a small symbol from the *'y-'* sounds. There is no need to memorize these characters if you can remember how to read and write a hybrid sound.

Compound kana with '-i' + 'y-' sounds tend to be associated with native Japanese words (kun'yomi). You will encounter some other, less common combination sounds, especially in words of foreign origin, but they can be considered exceptions to the rules above, and it is best to learn about those if and when you see them.

Combination Hiragana

	ya	yu	yo
k	きゃ kya	きゅ kyu	きょ kyo
s	しゃ sha	しゅ shu	しょ sho
t	ちゃ cha	ちゅ chu	ちょ cho
h	ひゃ hya	ひゅ hyu	ひょ hyo
m	みゃ mya	みゅ myu	みょ myo
n	にゃ nya	にゅ nyu	にょ nyo
r	りゃ rya	りゅ ryu	りょ ryo
g	ぎゃ gya	ぎゅ gyu	ぎょ gyo
j	じゃ ja/jya	じゅ ju/jyu	じょ jo/jyo
b	びゃ bya	びゅ byu	びょ byo
p	ぴゃ pya	ぴゅ pyu	ぴょ pyo

Long Vowels

Extended vowel sounds, such as *'-oo'* or *'-ee,'* are shown by adding a character or mark to the kana with the sound we need to double. They are called 長音 (*chouon*) in Japanese, and they are represented in different ways in each of the kana scripts. We can easily pronounce a long sound when talking, and the rules for writing them are not too difficult either.

When writing **hiragana**, we add one of three vowel characters for long vowel sounds *(writing them at normal size)*:

> For *'a'* sounds, it's an extra あ *(a)*
> For *'i'* **and** *'e'* sounds, add い *(i)*
> For *'u'* **and** *'o'* sounds, add う *(u)*

So, to extend the *'a'* part of か *(ka),* you add あ and write かあ *(ka-a)*. Similarly, to double the *'i'* in き *(ki),* you write きい *(ki-i)*. く becomes くう *(ku-u)*, and so on:

The popular examples showing the importance of correct pronunciation for long vowel sounds are to compare the Japanese spellings of 'grandfather' and 'uncle,' or 'aunt' and 'grandmother.' *(Your uncle or aunt may be offended if you refer to them as a grandparent!)*

おじさん
ojisan
"uncle"

おじいさん
ojiisan
"grandfather"

(the honorific title *'-san'* is added when using the respectful *Sonkeigo* speech)

In Romaji, long vowel sounds can be represented by either writing the vowels out in full or using a *macron* (a diacritic mark) A macron is just a line above a vowel that shows its sound is longer when pronounced, e.g., *'Tōkyō,'* pronounced as *'Toukyou.'*

Long Consonants

Also referred to as **double consonants**, we can write these sounds by adding a **'small tsu'** *(also called Sokuon)* between two kana. The consonant sound from a character that follows a small tsu should be heard twice when reading. It's the same in both kana scripts, using small つ and ツ symbols.

For example, a small つ between き*(ki)* and て *(te)* makes the word きって pronounced as *"ki-t-te,"* not *'ki-tsu-te'* or *'ki-te.'* It means 'postage stamp' and the kanji word is 切手:

While words with a *small tsu* may look very similar to others, and pronunciation might not seem to vary much, they are entirely different words.

Adding a small つ between the characters い and た of the word いた makes the word いった. Pronunciation of this word is neither いつた *('i-tsu-ta')* or いた *('i-ta')* but, instead, いった is pronounced as *"i-t-ta."* The small tsu inherits a *'t-'* sound from the character た *(ta)*:

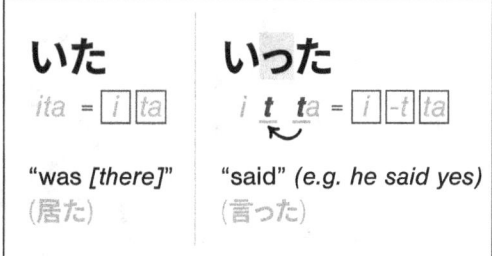

Small つ take one *mora* to pronounce, as though they were any other kana character, but they don't add an extra syllable sound. It can almost seem like you are stuttering when pronouncing words with double consonants. *The example above,* いった *might be spelled phonetically as "eet-ta." The extra 't' sound must be heard and squeezed into the same two morae as* いた *(i-ta)*.

Long consonants are *'unvoiced'* in pronunciation, including those that are usually modified by *dakuten and handakuten*. In other words, *'voiced'* consonants that follow a *small tsu* are pronounced as if they do not have dakuten.

There are few words where double consonant sounds have dakuten, and they tend to be limited to foreign loanwords - this means they will usually be found in the other kana script, katakana, as used in this example:

The word for 'bed' as ベッド *(beddo),* but the ド *(do)* keeps its original ト *(to)* sound, as though written ベット. It's pronounced as *'be-t-to,'* not *'be-d-do.'* This word takes three *morae* to say.

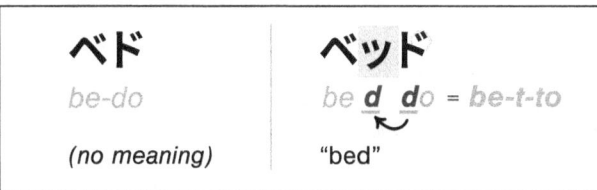

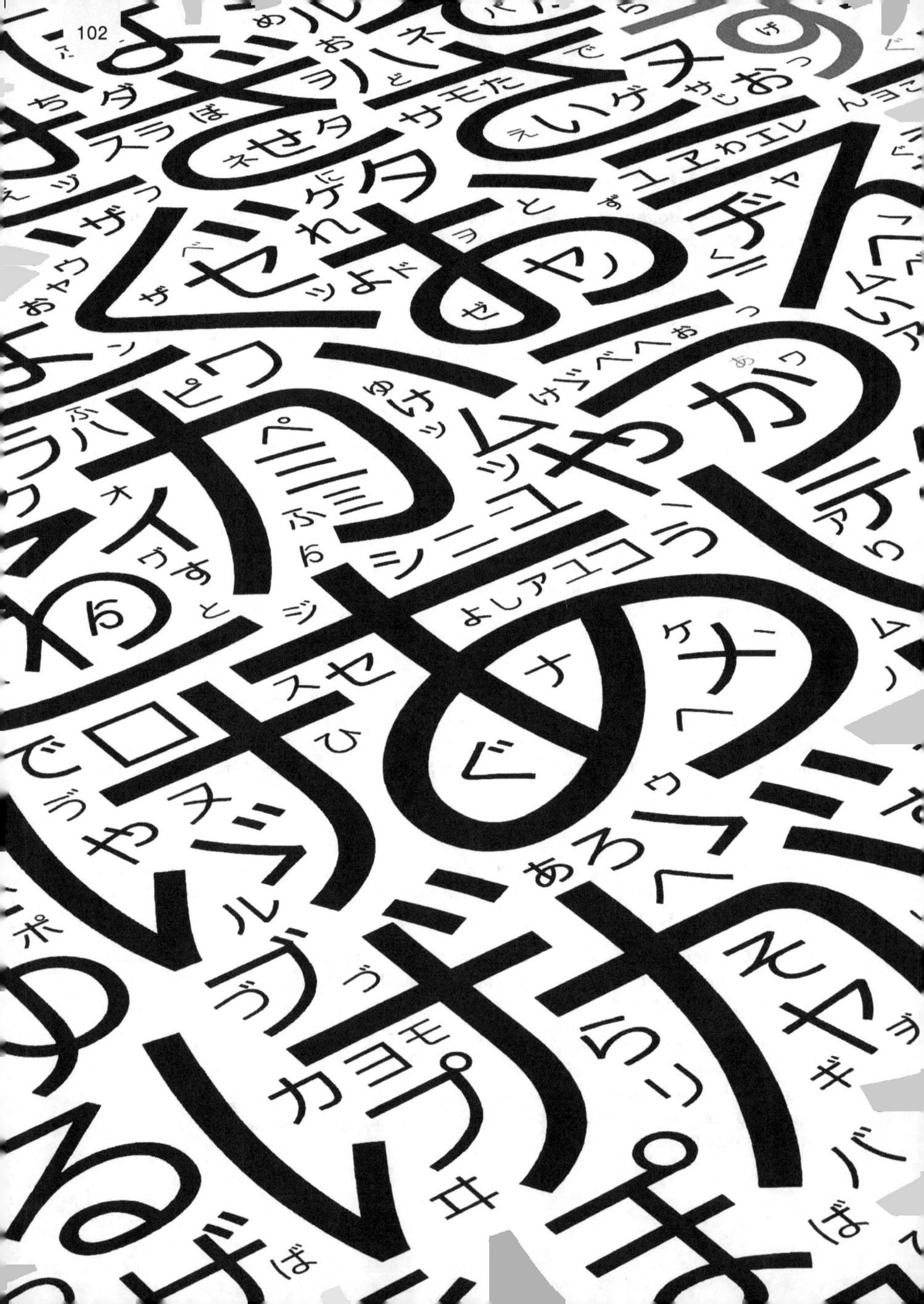

//////////////////////////////// **PART 4**

Study Tools

This section provides some additional tools to aid in your studies. These pages can be copied or cut out but may be used directly for writing on.

The following double-sided sheets contain additional grid templates that you can use for character writing practice. To begin with, these consist of larger 1-inch squares, followed by a section of more standard 0.7-inch squares. Each spread has a set with and without the dotted center guides.

Pages 144-146 provide an overview of the Japanese Language Proficiency Test (JLPT), which may be more or less useful, depending on what your goal is with Japanese. I wanted to include this as it may just help you to work out how far you wish to take your studies!

Pages 147-154 contain double-sided templates that readers can cut out to create a mini flashcard deck. These are helpful for revision and testing your memory of hiragana. They may not be as durable as authentic cards, but I felt it would be nice to include these to save you from additional expense. Each *'card'* features the kana sound or pronunciation hint and stroke order, along with some others to remind you of those critical sound change rules. You will also find some mini charts and spare, blank flashcards - *either for custom rules or if a card goes missing!*

Upon completion of the hiragana script, the next step on your journey into Japanese will be katakana. I have made a separate katakana workbook available, but both kana scripts are covered in the later books in this series - those covering the use of kanji and exploring how grammar is applied to the characters you are learning.

(Eventually, this series will consist of a more complete set of workbooks that even teach how to write groups of individual kanji characters, however, there are thousands of those so this is a work in progress!)

Writing Practice Template

(1-inch grid with guides)

Writing Practice Template

(1-inch grid without guides)

Writing Practice Template

(1-inch grid with guides)

Writing Practice Template

(1-inch grid without guides)

Writing Practice Template

Writing Practice Template

(1-inch grid with guides)

Writing Practice Template

(1-inch grid without guides)

Writing Practice Template

Learning Japanese Made Simple - by Dan Akiyama

(1-inch grid with guides)

Writing Practice Template

(1-inch grid without guides)   *Learning Japanese Made Simple - by Dan Akiyama*

Writing Practice Template

(1-inch grid with guides)

Writing Practice Template

(1-inch grid without guides)

Writing Practice Template

(1-inch grid with guides)

Writing Practice Template

(1-inch grid without guides)

Writing Practice Template

(1-inch grid with guides)

Writing Practice Template

(1-inch grid without guides)

Writing Practice Template

(1-inch grid with guides)

Writing Practice Template

(1-inch grid without guides)

Writing Practice Template

(1-inch grid with guides)

Writing Practice Template

(1-inch grid without guides)

Writing Practice Template

(1-inch grid with guides)

Writing Practice Template

(1-inch grid without guides)

Writing Practice Template

(0.7-inch grid with guides)

Writing Practice Template

(0.7-inch grid without guides)

Writing Practice Template

(0.7-inch grid with guides)

Writing Practice Template

(0.7-inch grid without guides)

Writing Practice Template

(0.7-inch grid with guides)

Writing Practice Template

(0.7-inch grid without guides)

Writing Practice Template

(0.7-inch grid with guides)

Writing Practice Template

(0.7-inch grid without guides)

Writing Practice Template

(0.7-inch grid with guides)

Writing Practice Template

(0.7-inch grid without guides)

Writing Practice Template

(0.7-inch grid with guides)

Writing Practice Template

(0.7-inch grid without guides)

Writing Practice Template

(0.7-inch grid with guides)

Writing Practice Template

(0.7-inch grid without guides)

Writing Practice Template

(0.7-inch grid with guides)

Writing Practice Template

(0.7-inch grid without guides)

Writing Practice Template

(0.7-inch grid with guides)

Writing Practice Template

(0.7-inch grid without guides)

Writing Practice Template

(0.7-inch grid with guides)

Writing Practice Template

(0.7-inch grid without guides)

About the JLPT

The Japanese Language Proficiency Test, known as 日本語の能力試験 in Japanese, or *Nihongo no nouryoku shiken*, is a system of standardized exams that are used to determine a person's linguistic ability with Japanese.

Formal certification is helpful for those who seek to study or work in Japan. Potential employers and universities may require a person to obtain a qualification at a basic level before allowing them to make an application. It's also popular amongst learners simply as a means of acknowledgment or checking personal progress with the language. Exams take place in July and December twice a year, either in Japan or overseas, at special test centers in certain countries.

JLPT is the non-Japanese speaker's equivalent to the 'TOEFL' *(Test of English as a Foreign Language)* or 'IELTS' *(International English Language Testing System)* for those who do not speak English. It consists of five levels of certification, beginning at N5 (the easiest level), certifying a basic understanding and use of the language, progressing up to N1 (the most difficult) aimed at those with fluency:

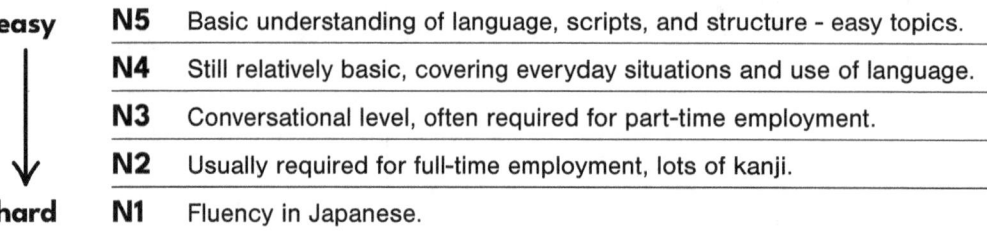

easy	**N5**	Basic understanding of language, scripts, and structure - easy topics.
	N4	Still relatively basic, covering everyday situations and use of language.
	N3	Conversational level, often required for part-time employment.
	N2	Usually required for full-time employment, lots of kanji.
hard	**N1**	Fluency in Japanese.

It's worth noting that the *Ministry of Education* and the *Japan Educational Exchanges and Services (JEES)* stopped publishing any *'Test Content Specifications'* in 2010 and learning from lists of vocabulary or kanji is discouraged. Instead, the JLPT website hosts a general summary of the competence needed for each level:

N5	The ability to understand some basic Japanese.
Reading	One is able to read and understand typical expressions and sentences written in hiragana, katakana, and basic kanji.
Listening	One is able to listen and comprehend conversations about topics regularly encountered in daily life and classroom situations, and is able to pick up necessary information from short conversations spoken slowly.

(Source: http://www.jlpt.jp/e/about/levelsummary.html - April 2022)

It may be useful and interesting to understand the requirements and assessment methods for the JLPT N5 level, whether you intend to study towards a formal qualification or not.

Although the summary table does not specify, a general knowledge of vocabulary and grammar is needed to satisfy the reading and listening requirements. The JLPT term for this is *'Language Knowledge,'* as shown in the N5 *'Composition of Test Items'* table below. This shows how the N5 examination is structured, highlighting the areas of knowledge required and how the exam will assess each:

Section + (time)		Test items	Purpose
Language Knowledge (20 min.)*	Vocabulary	Kanji reading	Test reading of words written in kanji
		Orthography	Test kanji and katakana for words written in hiragana
		Contextually-defined expressions	Test words whose meaning is defined by context
		Paraphrases	Test words and expressions with similar meaning
Language Knowledge Reading (40 min.)*	Grammar	Sentential grammar 1 (selecting grammar form)	Test judgment on grammar formats that suit sentences
		Sentential grammar 2 (sentence composition)	Test sentence composition that is syntactically accurate and makes sense
		Text grammar	Test judgment on suitability of sentences for text flow
	Reading	Comprehension (short passages)	Test understanding of contents by reading easy original text of approximately 80 characters regarding topics and situations involving study, everyday life and work
		Comprehension (mid-size passages)	Test understanding of contents by reading easy original text of approximately 250 characters regarding topics and situations in everyday life
		Information retrieval	Test ability to retrieve necessary information from original materials such as notices (approximately 250 characters)
Listening (30 min.)		Task-based comprehension	Test understanding of contents by listening to coherent text (test ability to extract necessary information to resolve specific issues and understand appropriate action to take)
		Comprehension of key points	Test understanding of contents by listening to coherent text (test ability to narrow down points based on necessary information presented in advance)
		Verbal expressions	Test ability to select appropriate verbal expressions by listening to circumstances while looking at illustrations
		Quick response	Test ability to select appropriate responses by listening to short utterances such as questions

(Source: https://www.jlpt.jp/e/guideline/testsections.html - April 2022)

The examination has three main parts: the first looks at your knowledge of vocabulary, including kanji words; the second explores your understanding of grammar rules, and then tests your ability to read and understand Japanese; and the third, final section tests the combination of all knowledge areas using audio recordings, in place of text.

*Before December 2020, test times for the first and second sections were 25 and 40 minutes, respectively.

Obtaining JLPT N5 certification requires an overall score of **80 points or more**, from a maximum available 180 marks. The *'reading'* section is worth twice as many points as the *'Listening'* section.

In addition, each of the two main sections now have a minimum score requirement, meaning low scores in either will result in failure, no matter how high a participant's final total is.

	Pts. Available for Section	Minimum Req. for Section
Language Knowledge (Vocabulary/Grammar) - Reading	0 - 120	38 / 120
Listening Section	0 - 60	19 / 120
Total Available	0 - 180	
N5 Pass (Minimum)	80 / 180	

(Source: http://www.jlpt.jp/e/guideline/results.html - April 2022)

JLPT N5 Requirements

The organizers of the JLPT no longer publish the specific vocabulary, grammar, and kanji knowledge requirements, so *'unofficial'* lists are all that you can find online. They suggest that all JLPT N5 questions and answers come from a pool of **800 vocabulary words** and **approximately 100 different kanji.** These figures cover more than a single exam requires but represent a **'safe' minimum level of knowledge.**

Fortunately, these vocabulary lists and kanji consist of simple, everyday, conversational Japanese, representing some of the most commonly used words. Topics include; numbers, dates, days, and time; family and friends; and common verb words *(such as walk, talk, read, write, and so on).*

The grammar requirements can also vary but include understanding and usage of common particles, *such as* は *(wa),* が *(ga), and* を *(wo),* and conjugation of the past and present tense - in both polite and informal speech.

Beginners with no knowledge may need to study for *up to 500 hours* before passing level N5 which equates to *less than 3 hours a day*, over a six-month period. When you consider that the JLPT exams consist of multiple-choice questions and answers, you *could* save a little time by learning only to *read* the kana scripts. However, unless you are in a rush for certification, an ability to write with kana is far too beneficial to skip. The recommended, longer-term strategy includes writing practice.

The examination process does not currently require a spoken test, making it possible to pass without talking at all - but conversations are a great way to learn and practice your Japanese, so they should not be overlooked entirely.

さ hiragana	か hiragana	あ hiragana
し hiragana	き hiragana	い hiragana
す hiragana	く hiragana	う hiragana
せ hiragana	け hiragana	え hiragana
そ hiragana	こ hiragana	お hiragana

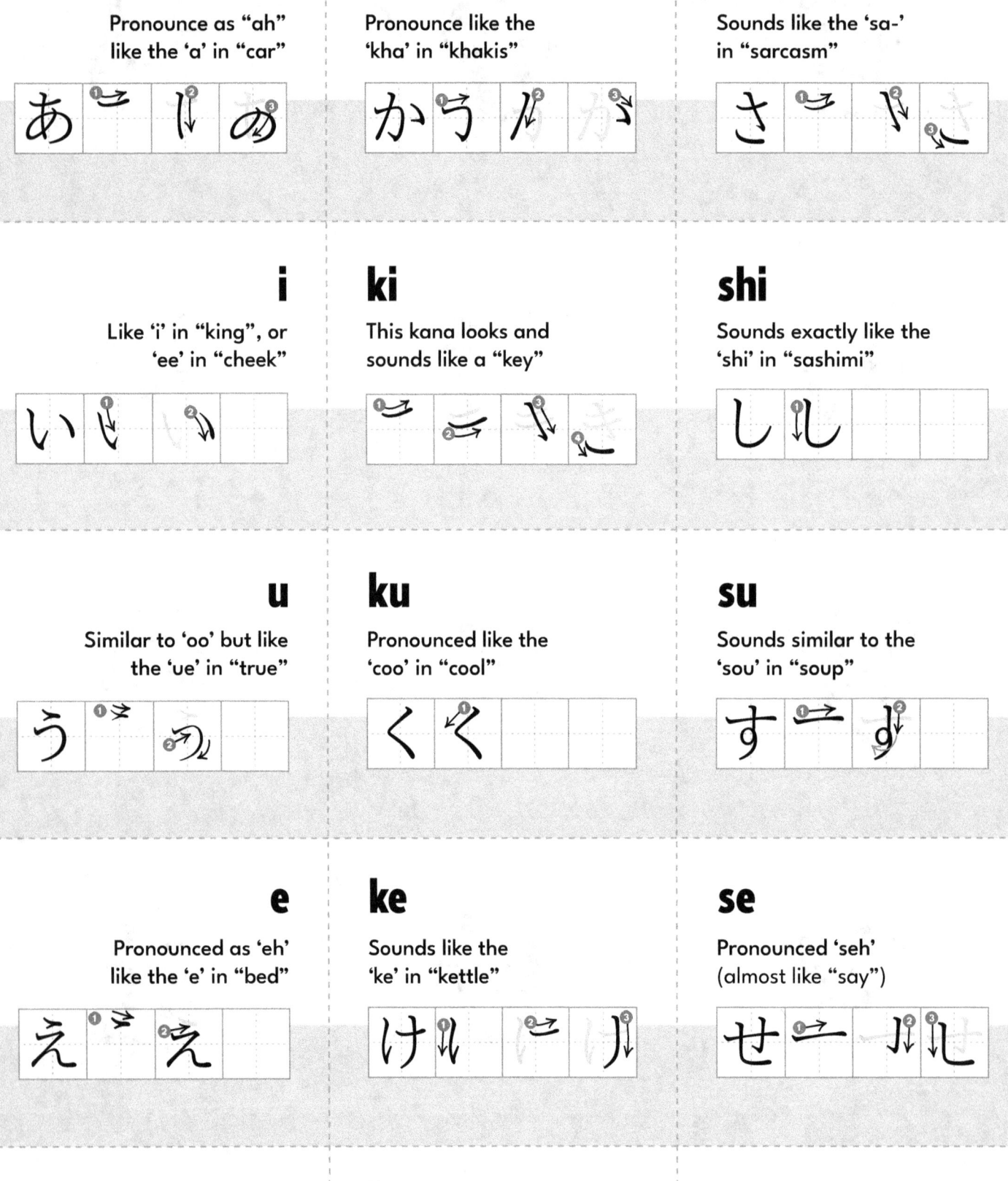

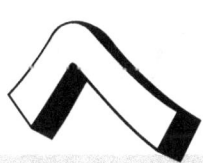  

ta
Sounds like the '-ta' in "Santa"

na
Sounds just like the '-na's in "banana"

ha
Pronounce as 'ha' like in "hand"

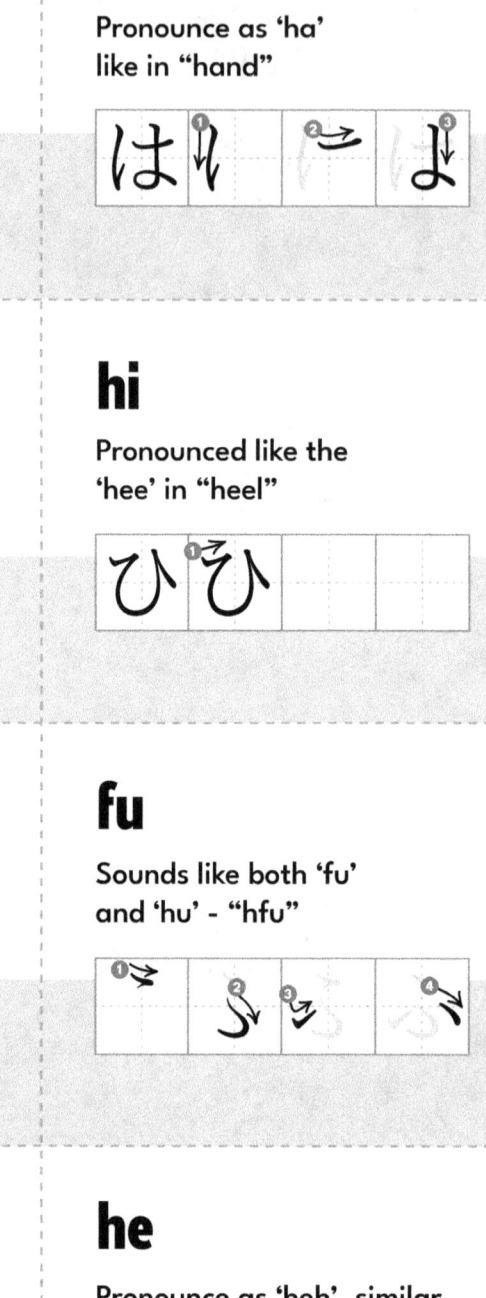

chi
Sounds just like the 'chee' in "cheeks"

ni
Sounds similar to the word "knee"

hi
Pronounced like the 'hee' in "heel"

tsu
Sounds like "two" and "Sue" combined

nu
Sounds like the 'noo' in the word "noon"

fu
Sounds like both 'fu' and 'hu' - "hfu"

te
Sounds like the 'te-' in "teddy bear"

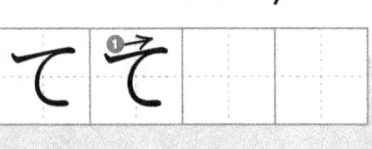

ne
Sounds like the 'ne' in the word "never"

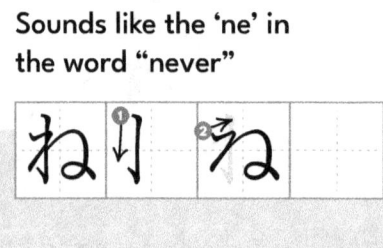

he
Pronounce as 'heh', similar to 'he' in "hello"

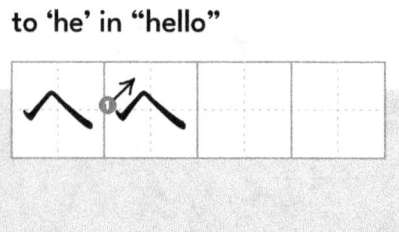

to
Sounds like the 'to-' in "tonic"

no
Sounds similar to the 'no' in "north"

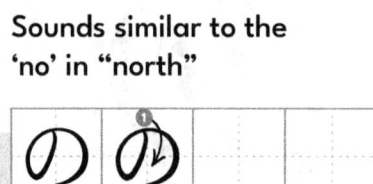

ho
Pronounce like the 'ho-' in "horse"

ma
Sounds like the 'ma-' in the word "man"

ya
Sounds much like the 'ya-' in "yak"

ra
Sounds a lot like the 'ra-' in "rabbit"

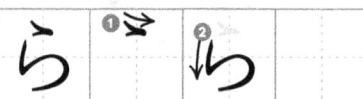

mi
Sounds just like the word "Me"

yu
Sounds just like the word "You"

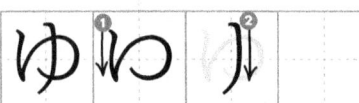

ri
Sounds a lot like the 'rea-' in "reach"

mu
Similar to the 'moo' in "moon"

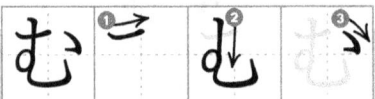

yo
Sounds like the 'yo' in "yogurt" and 'ya' in "yacht"

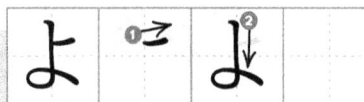

ru
Sounds like the '-ru' in "guru"

me
Sounds like the 'me-' in "men"

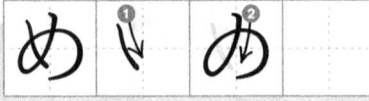

wa
Sounds like the 'wa-' in "wacky" or "wax"

re
Sounds like the 're' in "rest" and the 'ra-' in "race"

mo
Sounds similar to the 'mo-' in "monsoon"

n
Similar to the '-n' in "plane", or "nnn"

ro
Sounds like the '-rro' in "churro"

Hiragana Reference Sheet

spare	っ Small Tsu	を hiragana
spare	ああ Long Vowels	しゃ Compound Kana
spare	spare	ぽぱ Dakuten

Hiragana Chart

w	r	y	m	h	n	t	s	k	
わ wa	ら ra	や ya	ま ma	は ha	な na	た ta	さ sa	か ka	あ a
	り ri		み mi	ひ hi	に ni	ち chi	し shi	き ki	い i
ん n	る ru	ゆ yu	む mu	ふ fu	ぬ nu	つ tsu	す su	く ku	う u
	れ re		め me	へ he	ね ne	て te	せ se	け ke	え e
を wo	ろ ro	よ yo	も mo	ほ ho	の no	と to	そ so	こ ko	お o

a · i · u · e · o

WO
Pronounced as お
(like the O in "box")

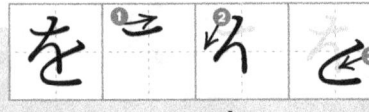

(を is a Particle)

Small tsu っ
= double consonant sound
(adds one mora)

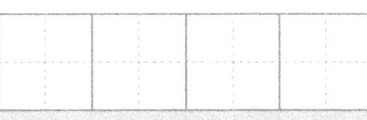

Regular kana '-i' + small kana 'y-'
e.g. し/き/ち + や/ゆ/よ

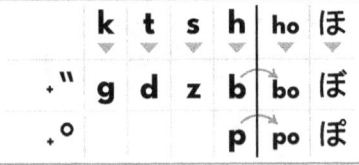

Double Vowels
Hiragana + extra vowel

[a] sounds + あ (a)
[i] / [e] sounds + い (i)
[u] / [o] sounds + う (u)

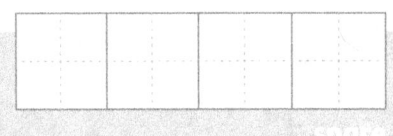

Kana with diacritic marks
= 'voiced' consonants
dakuten ゛ / handakuten ゜

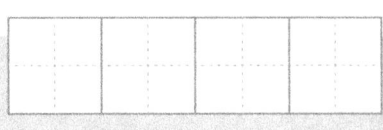

▲ Voiced Consonants
▼ Combination Kana

a	ぱ pa	ば ba	だ da	ざ za	が ga		
i	ぴ pi	び bi	ぢ ji/di	じ ji	ぎ gi		
u	ぷ pu	ぶ bu	づ zu/du	ず zu	ぐ gu		
e	ぺ pe	べ be	で de	ぜ ze	げ ge		
o	ぽ po	ぼ bo	ど do	ぞ zo	ご go		

ぴゃ pya	びゃ bya	じゃ ja/jya	ぎゃ gya	りゃ rya	にゃ nya	**ya**
ぴゅ pyu	びゅ byu	じゅ ju/jyu	ぎゅ gyu	りゅ ryu	にゅ nyu	**yu**
ぴょ pyo	びょ byo	じょ jo/jyo	ぎょ gyo	りょ ryo	にょ nyo	**yo**
みゃ mya	ひゃ hya	ちゃ cha	しゃ sha	きゃ kya		**ya**
みゅ myu	ひゅ hyu	ちゅ chu	しゅ shu	きゅ kyu		**yu**
みょ myo	ひょ hyo	ちょ cho	しょ sho	きょ kyo		**yo**

Answer Key

Check how you did in the reading exercises here:

Page 029					Page 037				
あう	au	あい	ai		あい	oi	あう	au
いえ	ie	あお	ao		うえ	ue	こえ	koe
おい	oi	ああ	aa		お	o	かく	kaku
うえ	ue	いい	ii		きく	kiku	おけ	oke
いう	iu	おう	ou		こけ	koke	かお	kao
					いけ	ike	あき	aki
					かう	kau	いう	iu
					えき	eki	あかい	akai
					いく	iku	あおい	aoi
					ここ	koko	きおく	kioku

Page 054					Page 068				
すし	sushi	とち	tochi		なに	nani	きぬ	kinu
つち	tsuchi	うた	uta		ほね	hone	ほし	hoshi
そと	soto	かた	kata		ぬの	nuno	ひと	hito
さけ	sake	しち	shichi		ひふ	hifu	のき	noki
こと	koto	さす	sasu		へた	heta	にし	nishi
くつ	kutsu	あした	ashita		はな	wana	はいく	waiku
かこ	kako	とおい	tooi		ふね	fune	かたな	katana
てつ	tetsu	きせつ	kisetsu		かに	kani	せいふ	seifu
せき	sato	さとい	satoi		ひな	hina	いのしし	inoshishi
たつ	tatsu	ちかてつ	chikatetsu		はし	washi	へいそつ	heisotsu

Page 080					Page 093				
やま	yama	むね	mune		わん	wan	さくら	sakura
ゆめ	yume	きもの	kimono		てら	tera	うちわ	uchiwa
よむ	yomu	さしみ	sashimi		つる	tsuru	まつり	matsuri
もも	momo	ゆかた	yukata		これ	kore	ほたる	hotaru
みや	miya	えまき	emaki		ふろ	furo	ふとん	futon
こめ	kome	みこし	mikoshi		のり	nori	れきし	rekishi
つゆ	tsuyu	うきよえ	ukiyoe		はる	haru	わふく	wafuku
むし	mushi	せともの	setomono		れい	rei	りろん	riron
まつ	matsu	すきやき	sukiyaki		しろ	shiro	ひのまる	hinomaru
うめ	ume				にほん	nihon	さむらい	samurai

Thank you.

First of all, congratulations on your progress with the Japanese language!

I hope that you found this first installment of my *Japanese Made Simple* series of workbooks useful and enjoyable. Thank you for choosing it from the wide selection of other titles that are available to buy. This series of books continues to be a labor of love and, hopefully, you will have found it easy to follow and full of practical, helpful information. If you enjoyed learning about the hiragana script in this way, consider looking at the second volume, covering the katakana script. Alternatively, some of the later editions feature all of the scripts and include more detailed information about kanji, grammar, and more!

The process of writing, designing and independently publishing books is both challenging and enjoyable. I make every effort to produce accurate language guides but it's easy to overlook little details here and there. Please let me know if you found any problems or mistakes in this book, so that I can promptly fix them for other readers.

Lastly, I wanted to ask you for a small favor...

It's incredibly satisfying to hear from people who are as keen about learning foreign languages as I am - especially when they have used one of my books. When you have a moment to spare, I would be grateful if you could consider leaving your feedback and a review on Amazon. We all rely on reviews to make our buying decisions, and your positive feedback is really helpful to *'the little guys'* and independent writers like me.

Let me know if there's anything I can do to improve my content and if there's anything else you would like to see in follow-up books. I look forward to hearing what you think!

Until next time, *arigatōgozaimasu!*

ありがとうございます!!
Dan.

Learning Hiragana (Japanese Made Simple)

Learn how to read, write and speak Japanese, with Hiragana

A Beginner's Guide and Integrated Workbook

Dan Akiyama

www.ingramcontent.com/pod-product-compliance
Lightning Source LLC
Chambersburg PA
CBHW081709100526
44590CB00022B/3714